Drawing Statues

Giovanni Civardi

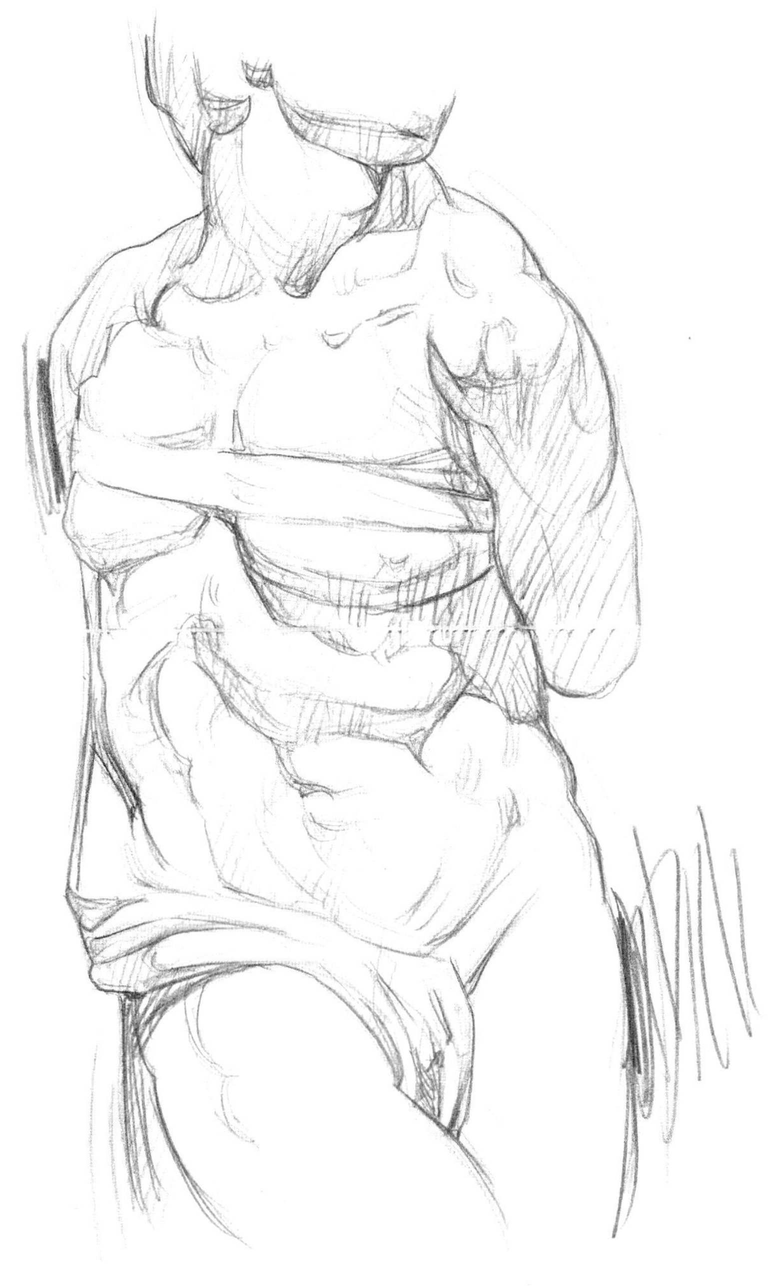

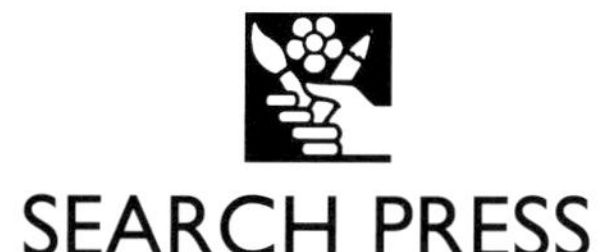

SEARCH PRESS

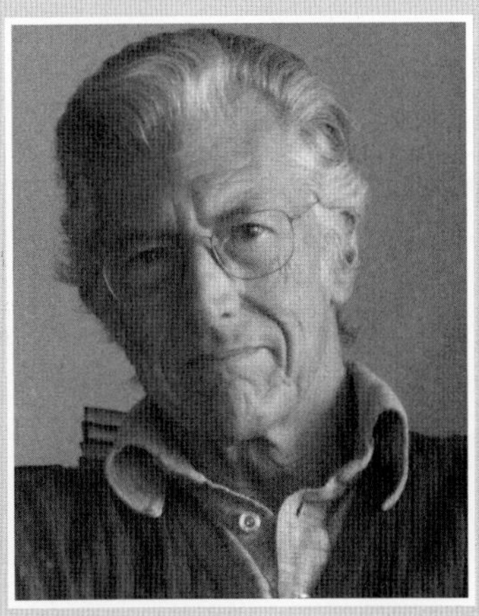

Giovanni Guglielmo Civardi was born in Milan in 1947. He dedicated himself to illustration, painting and sculpture for many years before focusing on anatomy for the artist and becoming a teacher of figure drawing.

To Vanessa, the source of the final question.
Matter feels the soul.
Human beings are like waves, similar to each other but never the same.
Joy is talkative, pain is silent.

First published in Great Britain in 2017 by
Search Press Limited, Wellwood, North Farm Road, Tunbridge Wells, Kent TN2 3DR

Originally published in Italy by Il Castello Collane Techniche, Milano

English translation by Burravoe Translation Services

ISBN: 978-1-78221-315-4

Printed in Malaysia

CONTENTS

In art, only that which has character is beautiful.

Auguste Rodin

To take something apart is to know it better, to go beyond mere appearances.

Rafael Mandressi

INTRODUCTION

In memory of my mother, Anselma Marchi (1914–2009), on the centenary of her birth.
Giovanni Civardi

'There is a huge difference between seeing something without a pencil in your hand, and seeing it while drawing it', wrote Paul Valéry at the start of his famous book *Degas Dance Drawing*. Drawing, really, is a tool that everyone can use, at least if limited to a primary aim, i.e. to see and understand the shapes and structures and, in particular, to recognise them. When you decide to draw an object, you realise that you are forced to observe in a completely different way to how you usually would: you have to pay more attention in order to really see it. It is the very act of drawing that sharpens the ability to observe, making you examine fundamental, characteristic aspects of the object that seem essential and sufficient for tracing a kind of portrait.

Drawing is a process that originates in curiosity. Drawing is looking to examine the structure of appearance; really seeing. This is the first real step towards drawing; the technical details, while important for developing the graphic and aesthetic qualities, are secondary, and concern over mastering them should not take precedence over the freshness of careful, direct, straightforward, almost naïve observation. Everyone can learn basic drawing, just as we can learn to speak a language or play a musical instrument. Of course, talent and favourable circumstances also help in creating art, but in order to know how to see, only a few requisites are necessary: the will to learn, constant practice, the precision of the outline, commitment and attention during execution and care taken over the tools used.

Drawing comprises just a few fundamental steps: looking at the object, for example, creating the outline and shape (direction in space, proportional ratios, structural elements and the extension of shadows or intensity of tones); and processing and storing this information for the short but necessary time it takes for the hand to transfer that information on to the sheet.

The drawing of sculptures has been popular[1] since the Renaissance and it has regularly been included in teaching programmes at art schools from the 16th century to the start of the 20th century. Attention was given mainly to ancient sculptures, in particular Greek ones, which are known largely by surviving Roman copies. These were considered as classics and perfect examples of the highest standards of beauty, style, harmony and composition. At art schools in the late 19th century (and in many of our modern-day ones too), the study of classic sculptures appears to be, while not totally absent or rejected (in observance of current aesthetic and cultural standards), certainly not overly incumbent. It was considered mainly as an educational reference to a high style in assuming the human figure. Most of all, these days, it is viewed as a way of learning a solid technical drawing technique and thorough anatomical knowledge, taught with anatomical-morphological comparison between the natural living model and the ancient classical shapes shown in art.

Many modern artists have practised drawing ancient sculptures and found it useful – and not just the ones representing the human body (such as Auguste Rodin or Medardo Ross) but also artists who, while finding inspiration from the human shape and condition, have interpreted the body to the limits of abstraction.

Alberto Giacometti, more than anyone, insisted that it is 'necessary to copy', 'to copy the past', not to create formal slavish reproductions, but because this is the best way to realise what you are seeing. Copying a work of art means reliving, comparing and repeating from the inside the process of its creation, its formal structure and composition and its style analysis or summary as carried out by the artist, to reach that degree of understanding and expression of reality.

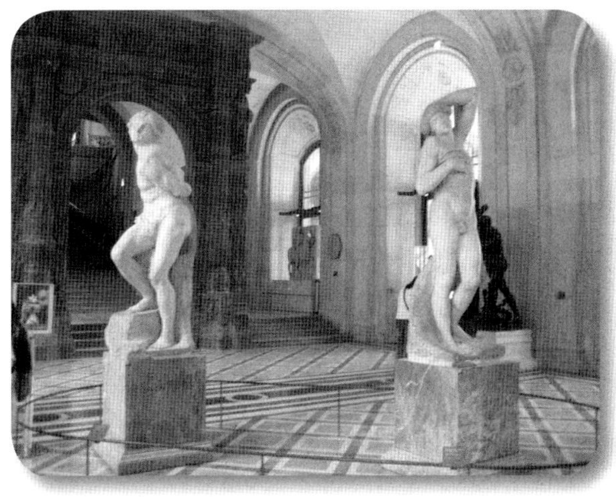

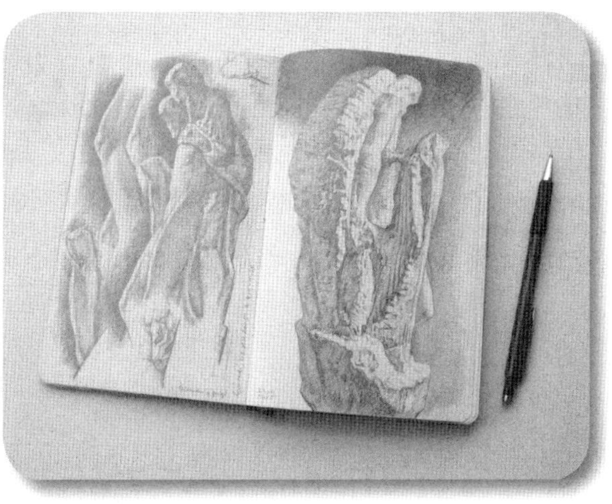

1 Almost all the drawings reproduced here (up to page 47) are sketches drawn with HB and 2B graphite on paper (21.5 x 27.5cm/ 8½ x 11¼in) and drawn directly from original statues, in the various museums, according to the lighting, distance and time conditions available (see page 48). The photographs used to accompany each statue were taken in the same conditions and in observance of the rules issued by each museum (no use of flash, stable support, etc.), which partly explains the poor quality of some of the images.

THEORETICAL AND PRACTICAL CONSIDERATIONS

Each drawing contains the first step in a journey of discovery by posing the question of how to represent what the eye sees. Anyone who has a naïve, curious attitude and wants to take a few drawing tools out for exploring, is on this same journey. Here are a few practical considerations:

- The design of the drawing has a descriptive function and highlights the important aspects of directly observing the subject, then choosing the most effective interpretation of it. The preferred method is pencil on paper, placing the subject in the central area of the sheet, isolated from the background, with an indication of scale, reference used, explanatory notes and clarifying details, etc.
- There is a difference between the academic copy from ancient times (plaster moulds etc.) and drawing from an original sculpture, in the environment in which it is kept or exhibited. The latter requires adapting to the available time and conditions, and this also creates greater empathy in observing the structure, balance, profile, volumes, relations with the surrounding environment, tonal planes and main axes, and the anatomical and morphological highlights.
- Creating a drawing allows gradual observation over time which can be interrupted or made hesitant through doubt and uncertainty of perception: it therefore stimulates questions, explanations and interpretations. Drawing is understanding; it is a guide to a different approach that pays more attention to reality; it is an integral part of the entire observation process and creates the foundations for a consistent verbal description. A drawing is not a servile copy of what is being looked at (even though it may be finicky and punctilious), but an interpretation of it, and, above all, a personal explanation of it.
- Drawing commits you to a continuous flow, coming and going between the observer and the observed object. It establishes comparative ratios between what you see and what you draw, and allows you to extract the most relevant and useful elements from a complex situation to guide graphic choices.
- **The support:** blank sketchbooks or notebooks are better than loose sheets, as they are bound with a hard cover, allowing you to draw freehand even when you do not have anything to lean on. Some notebooks have the advantage of being pocket-sized or medium-sized (15 x 20cm/6 x 7¾in approximately) and therefore easy to carry around.
- **The tools:** an observational drawing must be carried out rapidly but carefully and precisely. Ballpoint pens (of various colours) can be used, or even felttip pens, but the ideal tool is still a medium-soft (HB) graphite pencil. Ordinary pencils can also be used, such as the ones with the graphite enclosed in a wooden casing, as can the thin graphite 'leads' that are inserted into propelling pencils, which are fragile but do not require sharpening. Any additional tools are minimal: it can be useful to have a plastic eraser (not to erase errors but to clean the paper of superfluous traces of graphite); and a metal paper holder to hold the pages in the notebook together while drawing.
- **Environment:** drawing in a museum requires suitable conduct, for example, working in silence, not blocking access for other visitors and not taking up public space. Sometimes it is wise to notify the museum wardens of what you are doing or ask them for permission beforehand. This applies especially to some art museums (the ones in which drawing is considered the equivalent of taking photographs), or in places where temporary exhibitions are held that are subject to copyright. Most museums allow photography in ambient lighting conditions (without the use of flash). It is therefore appropriate to take some photographs of the sculpture, after drawing it, so that you have a record for any further study and to realise which inevitable alterations have been created by the optical characteristics of the camera lens on the perspective and shape of the sculpture, when comparing the photograph with the drawing or sketch.

And lastly, expect a few difficulties regarding, for example:

- **Lighting** (of the room or the sculpture), which is not always suitable for highlighting the formal elements that the drawing artist is interested in. Natural daylight may be weak, while artificial light may be diffused. There may be several light sources or the source may be too concentrated, which can create deep shadows or unnecessary reflections, depending on the type of material used to create the sculpture, such as bronze with a light or dark patina, marble, plaster or terracotta. Reflection from the cases protecting small sculptures in museums may also interfere with viewing the artwork.
- **Distance or observational perspective**: rather frequently it is not possible to observe the sculptures easily from the most suitable points of view and they are different when walking around the work of art. The view you get may be a compulsory one. This happens in museums but also with open-air monuments, which are almost always located in public places and in an elevated position, too far or too uncomfortable for a long period of drawing.

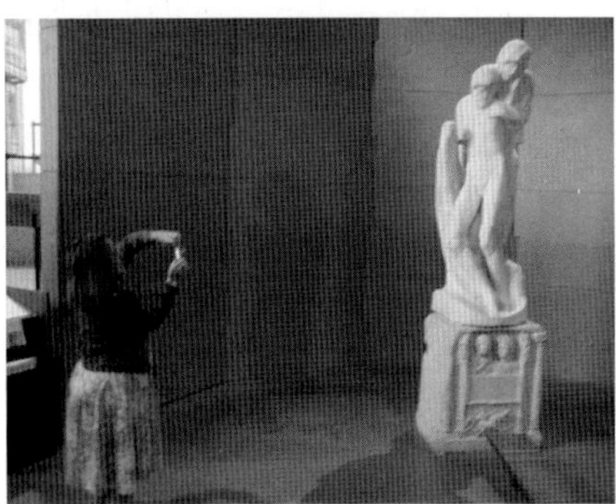

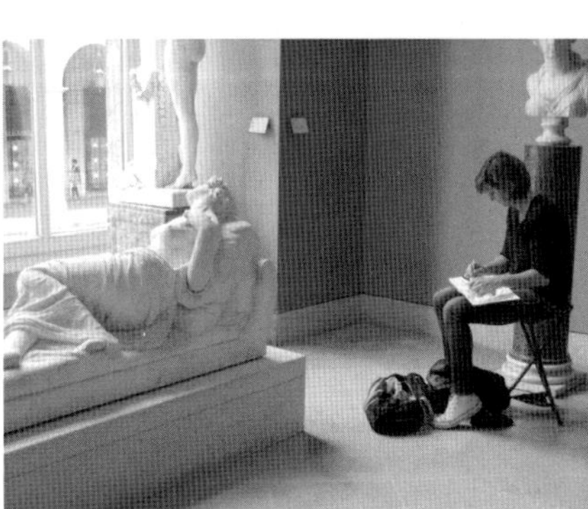

Some people take photographs, while others draw…

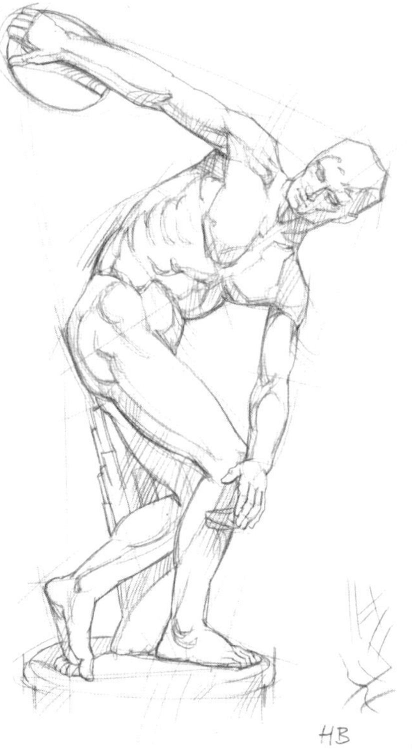

Line drawing (structure)

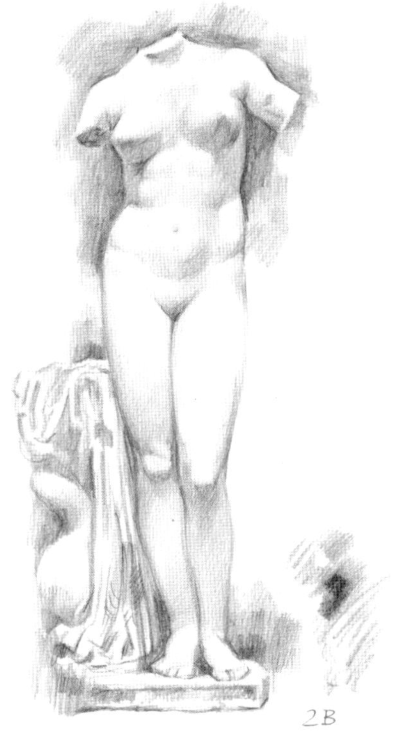

Tonal drawing (modulation)

Line drawing provides for precision when defining the structure, profiles, planes etc. of the form being drawn. Line drawing is carried out using a suitable tool such as pen or pencil for tracing thin, clear marks and outlining the tonal areas, identifying the main axes, marking the profiles and creating multiple facets of the tonal planes by using straight lines.

Tonal drawing, on the other hand, is suited to identifying light and shade areas, maintaining a more natural process of visual perception, where the line is only established by the edges where the tones of varying intensity meet. Fill in the tonal areas using blunt and soft drawing tools such as soft graphite or charcoal and blend the various tones into each other. The two methods, line and tonal, can be used together.

How to proceed[1] The observation drawing is basically a sketch carried out rapidly and succinctly. It has different aims and aspects from an artistic drawing (in fact, to draw it you do not need to know how to draw well) and therefore it is not easy to break it down into separate phases of execution. However, it is necessary to start putting marks down on the paper at some point. For example, you can begin with a light marking of the space that the image of the subject will occupy on the sheet (think of the maximum height, maximum width, overall shape, etc.), and then continue with an indication of the position and reciprocal proportion of the main parts of it, ending with an analysis of the most important structural details. Clearly, before beginning the drawing, you must choose the most suitable, effective and practical point of view for studying the subject.

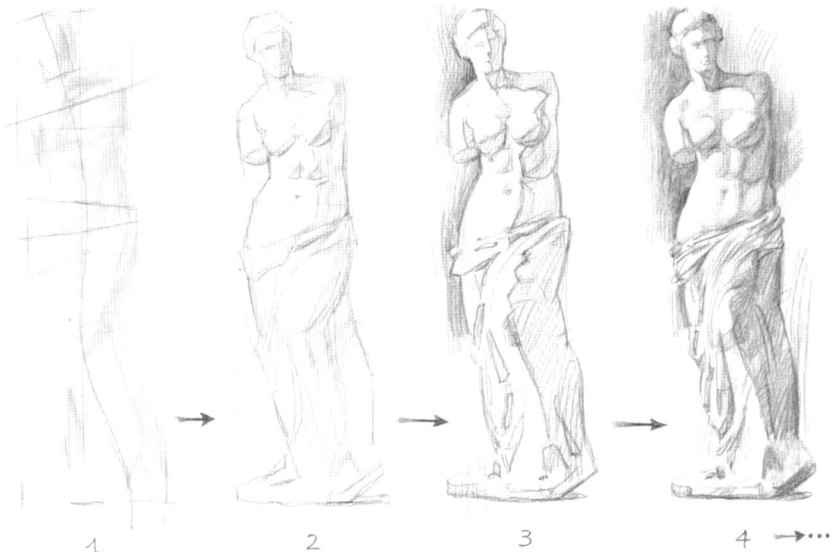

Phase 1 – Linear outline

Phase 2 – Separation of the light areas from the shade areas

Phase 3 – Execution of the tonal planes

Phase 4 – Graduation of the tones and addition of accents of light and shade

1 For more information about how to draw the human figure, you can also consult my previous book: *An Introduction to Drawing the Human Body* by Giovanni Civardi, Search Press, 2014

MARSYAS

Myron (5th century BC), Marsyas, *Roman copy in marble from the Greek original, perhaps in bronze, from the mid-fifth century BC, height 159cm (62¾in). Rome, Vatican Museums.*

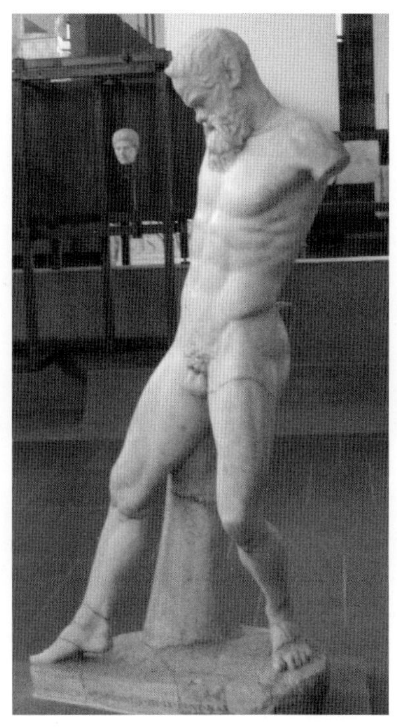

Ancient Greek sculptures focused on the human body are known almost entirely by the marble copies created by Roman artists to decorate Patrician homes. Most of the originals were cast in bronze and almost all have been lost. Stone ones were painted in bright colours relating to the characteristics of the area in which they were exhibited. The original bronze works were often copied in other materials such as marble, sometimes in different sizes, and special expedients were required to compensate for the greater fragility of marble compared with metal, such as placing drapes and vines on the figure to support the body in an upright position and avoid breakage of delicate parts. The figure of *Marsyas* is the remaining fragment of a group that also included Athena, portraying the mythical story of the invention of the double flute.

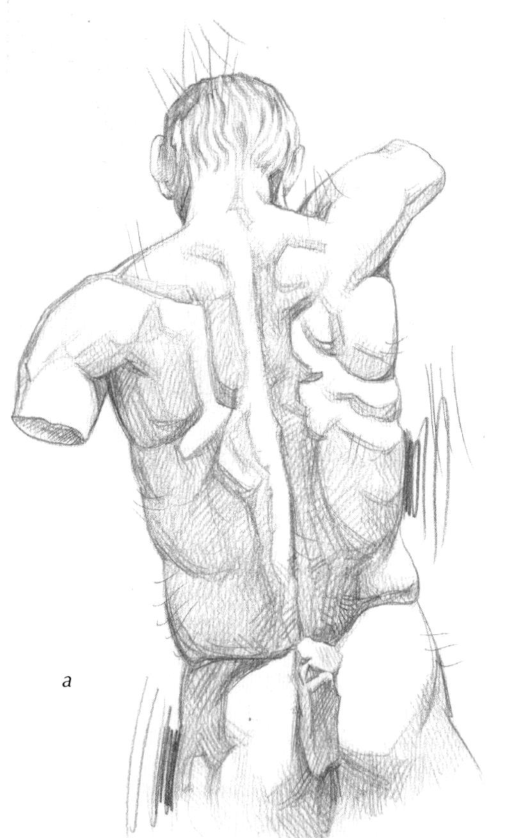

Marsyas was a 'satyr', a genie of the woods, who had long ears and a tail: there is only a part of this remaining at the base of the spine (a).

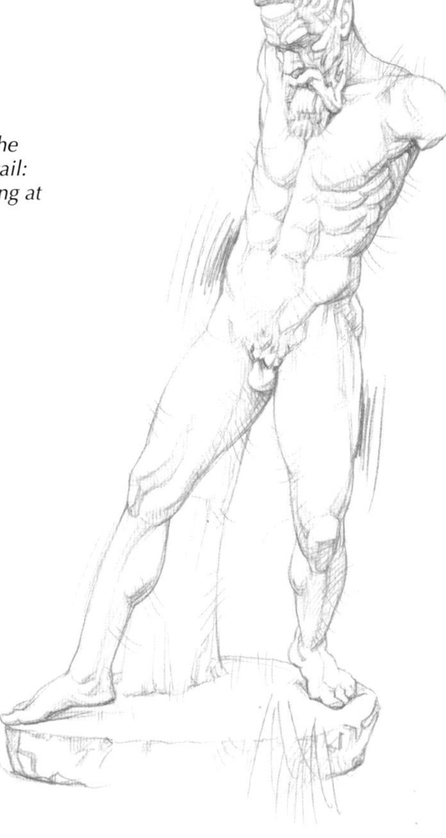

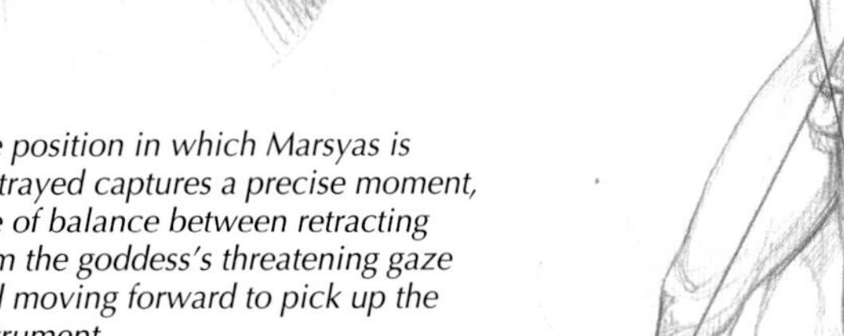

The position in which Marsyas is portrayed captures a precise moment, one of balance between retracting from the goddess's threatening gaze and moving forward to pick up the instrument.

b

The most expressive view of the figure (which must be imagined with his right arm lifted up to protect his face and the left one detached from the body) is the one that highlights the triangular compositions (b) and the muscular tension of the thigh and left leg, which supports the entire body and concludes the movement.

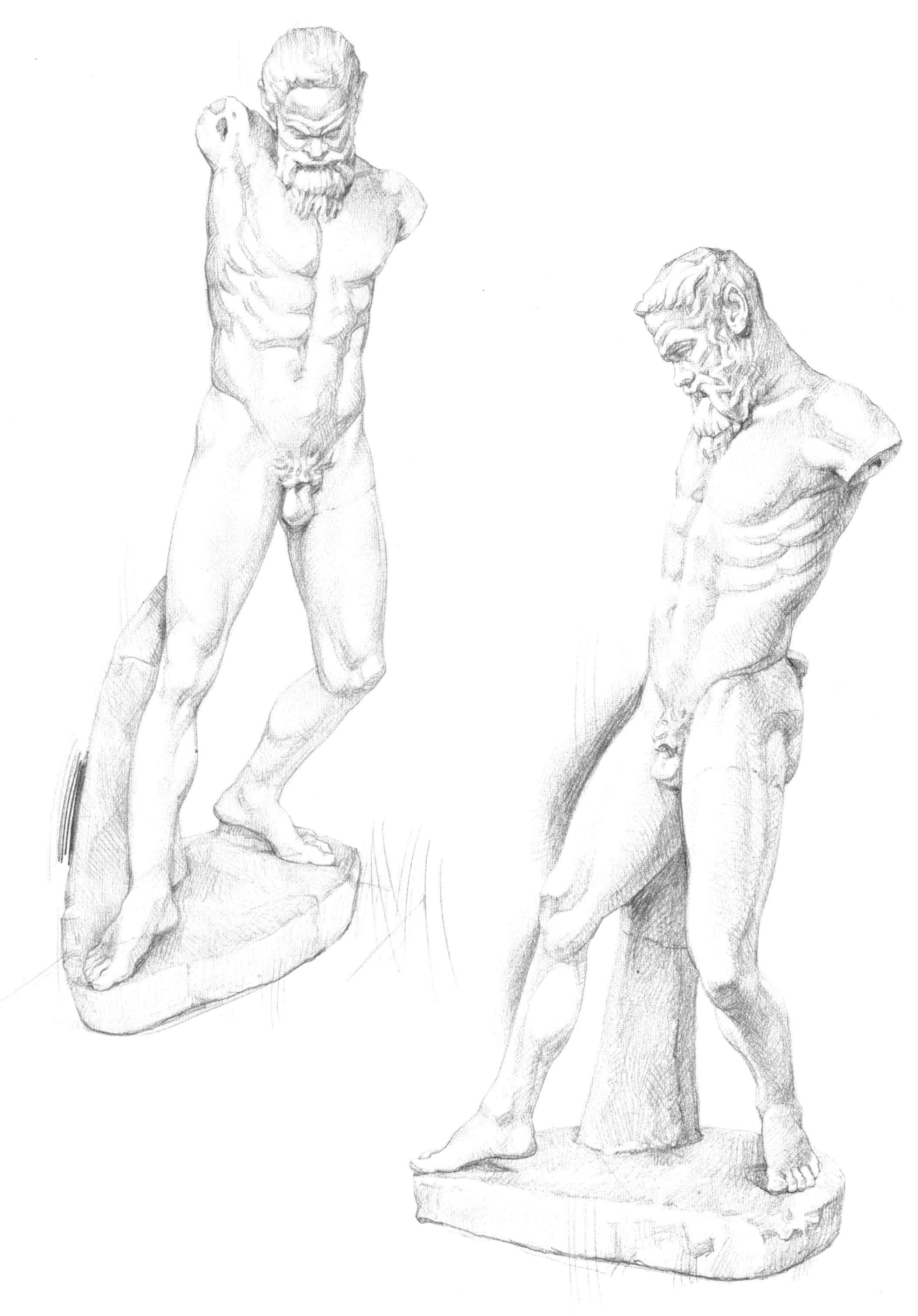

DORYPHOROS

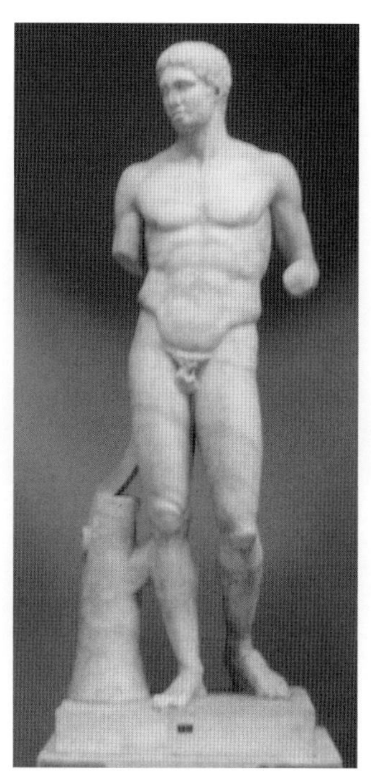

Polykleitos of Argos (5th century BC), Doryphoros, *a Roman copy in marble from the Greek original in bronze, from 440 BC, height 200cm (79in). Rome, Vatican Museums. (An almost complete copy of better quality is kept in the National Archaeological Museum in Naples.)*

The statue is of a spear holder, a figure who originally held a heavy spear (*dòry*) that was supported by the left hand and rested on the corresponding shoulder.

The figure overall is calm, but an impression of tension comes from the harmonious and unequal distribution of the body weight on the legs, so as to create a *contrapposto* (or counterpose). The sculpted body finds a dynamic balance using the composition of contrasting shape and tensions: the bending of the left arm contrasts with the straight right leg, while the left leg, which is free and bent, contrasts with the right hand, which is straight and close to the body. Consequently, the cross axes at the shoulders and pelvis are not horizontal, but sloping sideways and in the opposite direction (a). The head is directed towards the side of the supporting leg, highlighting the left-hand sternocleidomastoid muscle, while the body is slightly rotated in the opposite direction.

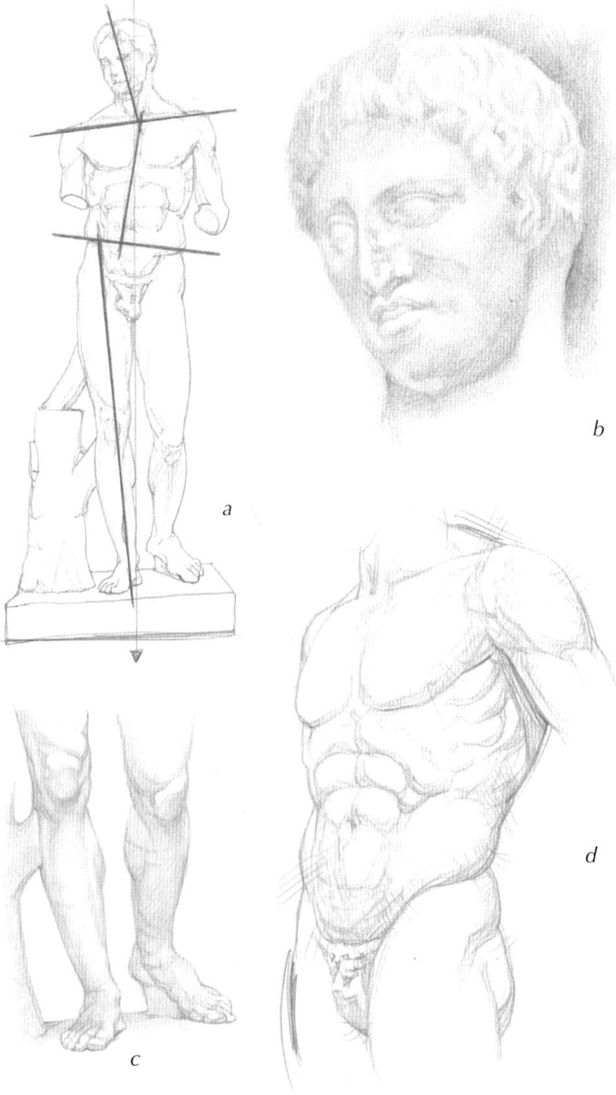

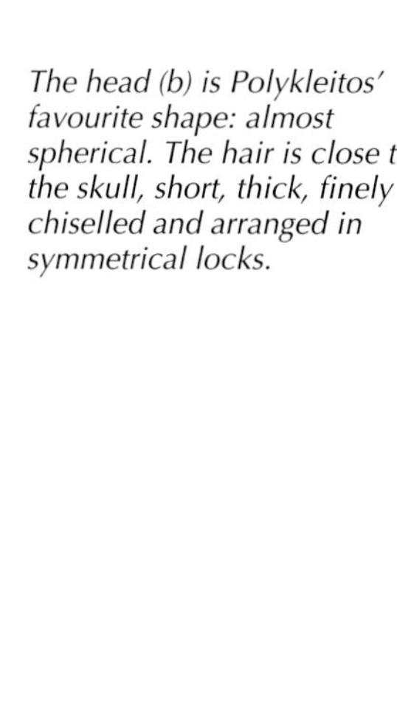

The head (b) is Polykleitos' favourite shape: almost spherical. The hair is close to the skull, short, thick, finely chiselled and arranged in symmetrical locks.

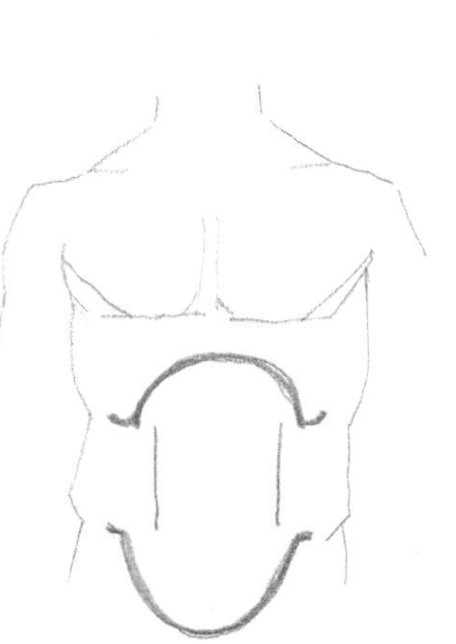

The rib vault and the inguinal arch (d) form the two semicircular, almost symmetrical limits of the abdominal 'armour' – a frequent stylistic character in ancient sculpture, which tends to highlight the torso's well distributed and accented muscles.

The right foot (c) is placed firmly flat on the ground, while the other is partly lifted, with only the toes resting on the ground; it is used to maintain balance and suggest a majestic stride. The left leg is bent and the pelvis on the same side is thus lower, causing a different level and aspect of each knee, with the left one further forward.

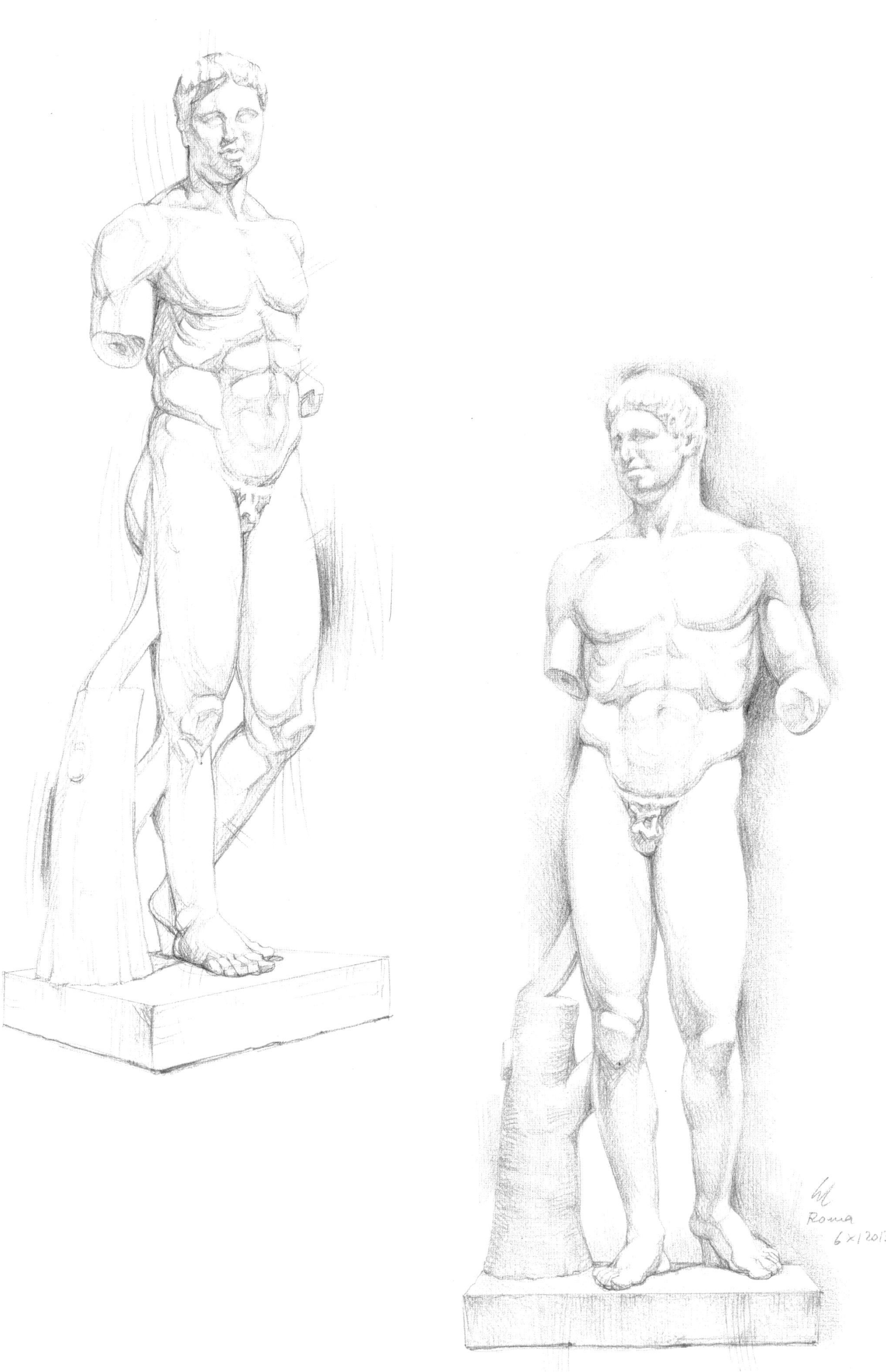
Roma
6 X 2013

APHRODITE OF CNIDUS

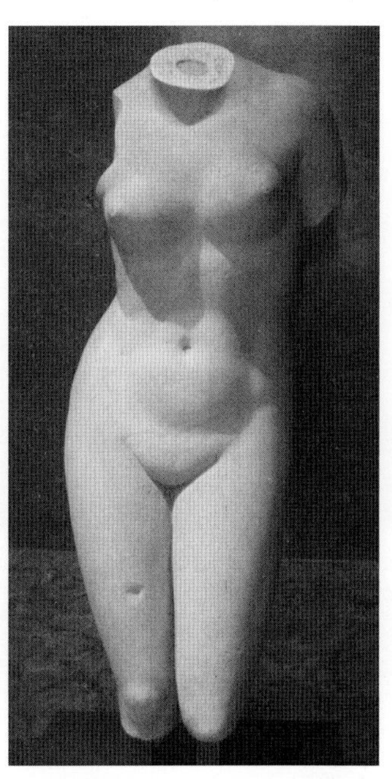

Praxiteles (4th century BC), Aphrodite of Cnidus, *Roman copy in marble from the Greek original dated 350 BC, height 105cm (41½in). Paris, Musée du Louvre.*

The *Aphrodite* (or *Venus*) *of Cnidus* by Praxiteles has been the inspiration for several copies and variations of stance since the time when the original was sculpted. The *Capitoline Venus* can also be traced back to it (see page 12). The most complete, best quality Roman copy (a) is kept at the Vatican Museums: the goddess is portrayed while she prepares to bathe, *contrapposto* (in counterpose) and completely nude, for the first time in Greek sculpture, which preferred to reserve nudes for the male figure only. The copy that I drew at the Louvre is a wonderful example of this type of subject: it is a fragment, concentrating solely on the torso, but is even more attractive for this reason. By drawing it from different points of view (except from the rear, as the statue stands almost next to the wall) it is possible to grasp the softness of the anatomical forms and, above all, the delicacy of the tonal planes.

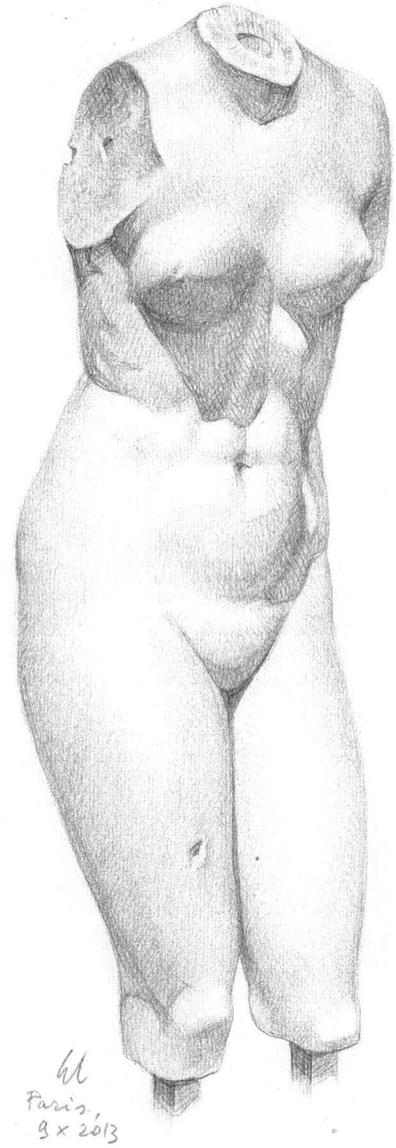

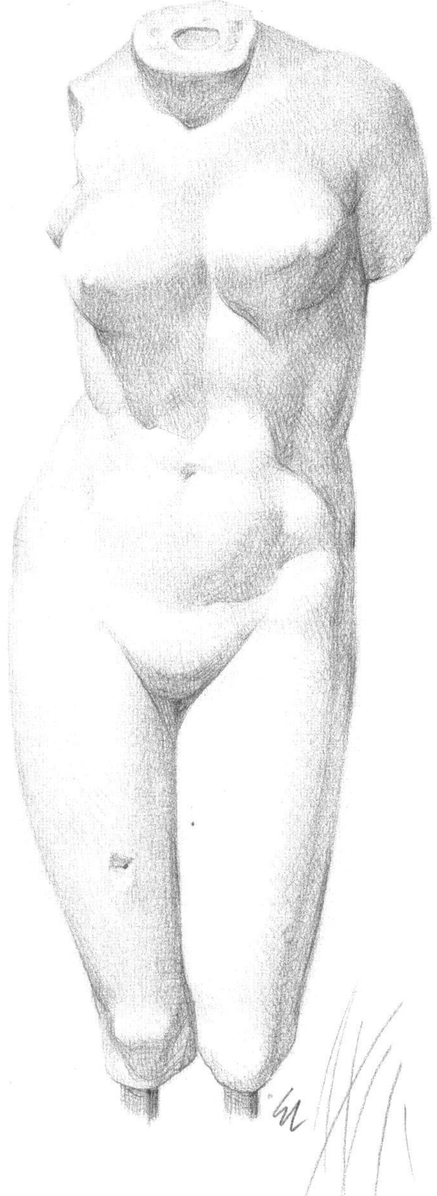

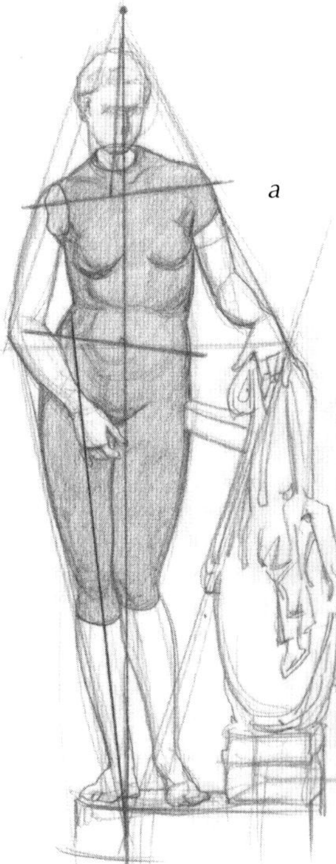

a

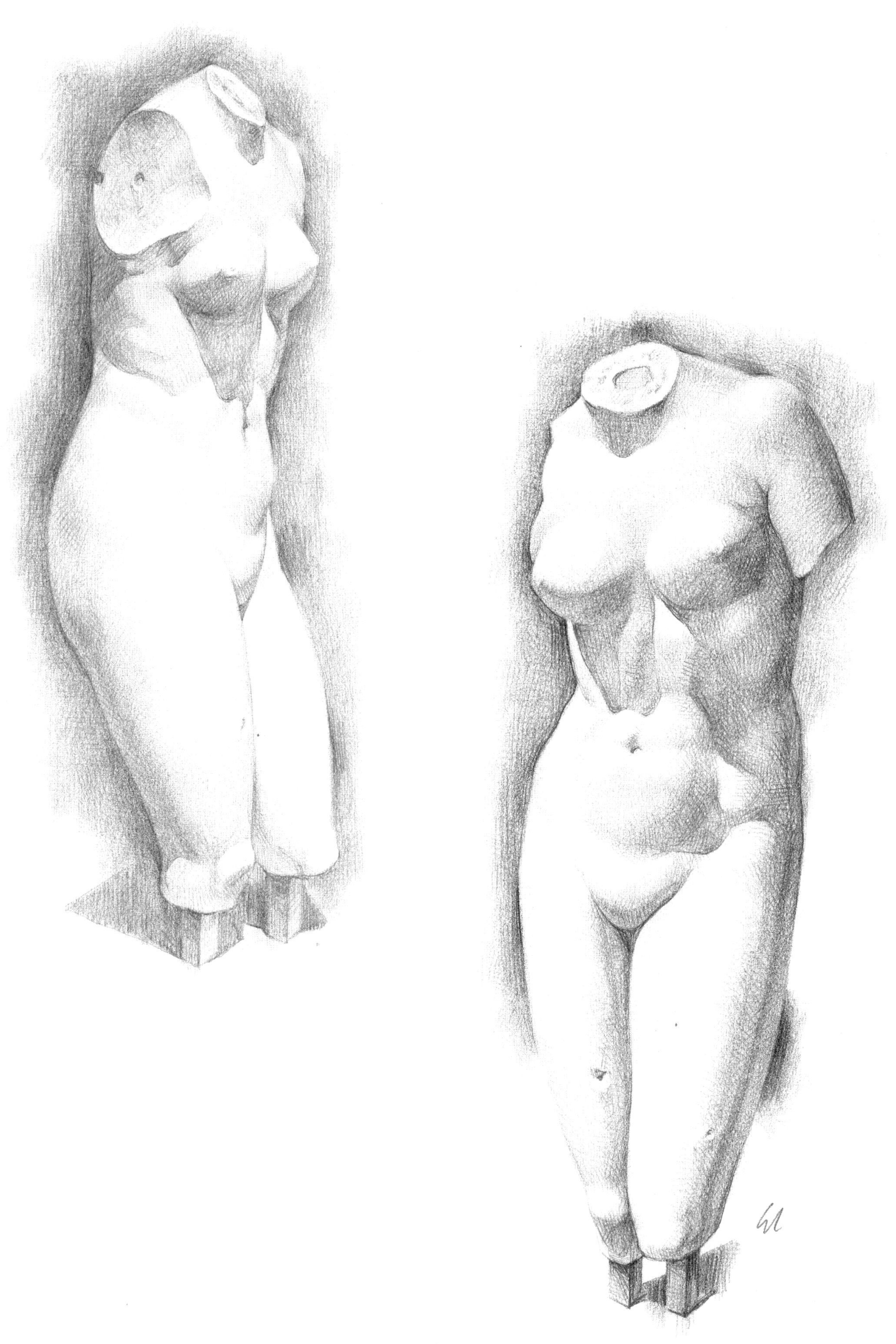

CAPITOLINE VENUS

Capitoline Venus, *a Roman copy in marble from a Greek original dated to the 3rd or 2nd century BC, in turn inspired by the* Aphrodite of Cnidus *by Praxiteles, circa 350 BC. Paris, Musée du Louvre.*

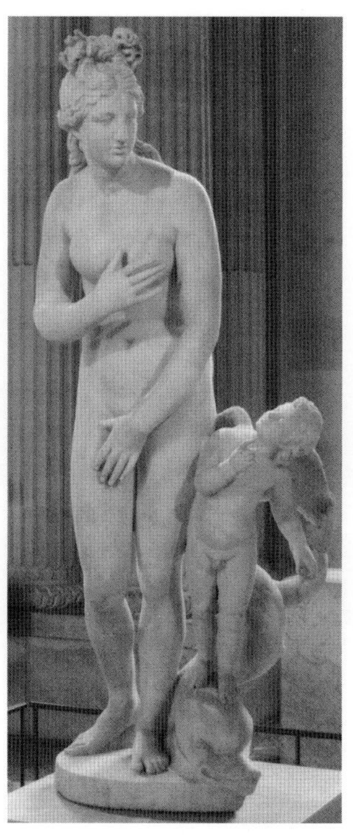

Capitoline Aphrodite, *a Roman copy in marble from a Greek Late Hellenistic model dated to the 3rd or 2nd century BC, height 176cm (69½in). Rome, Capitoline Museums.*

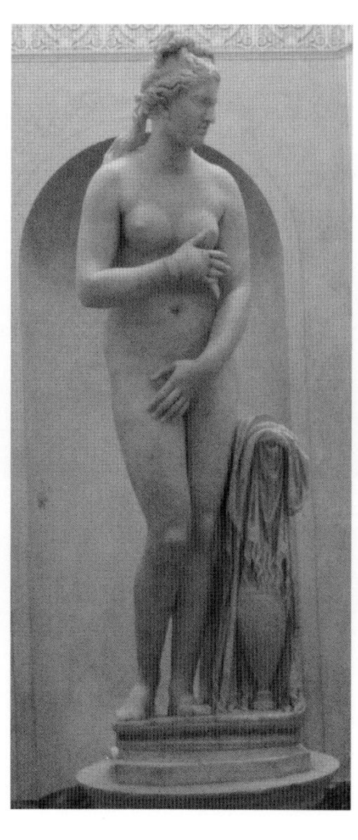

The style of the so-called *Capitoline Venus* has some striking similarities with that of the *Aphrodite of Cnidus* from which it originates (see page 10), but it also shows a few intimistic variations – in other words, hints of a familiar or domestic scene. For example, the overall manner is almost curled up, the body modestly hidden by the movement of the hands and bending forwards a little, to protect herself further. If the opportunity arises, it is interesting to compare the two different copies taken from the same inspiring model, appreciating likenesses and variations, as I did in this case.

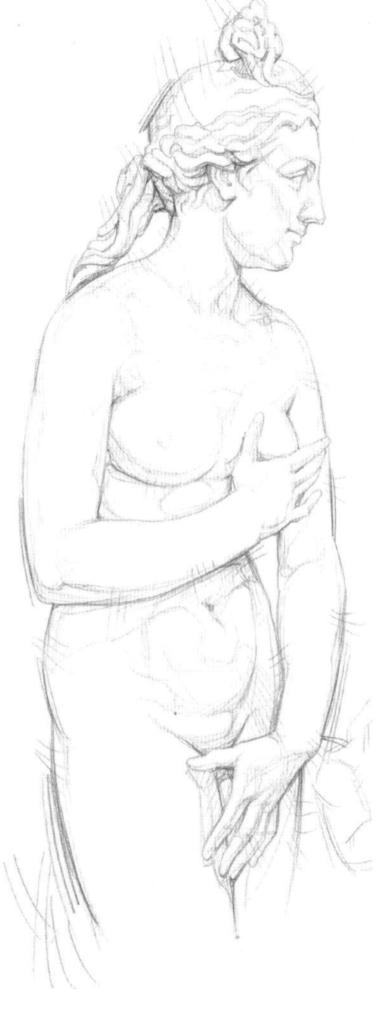

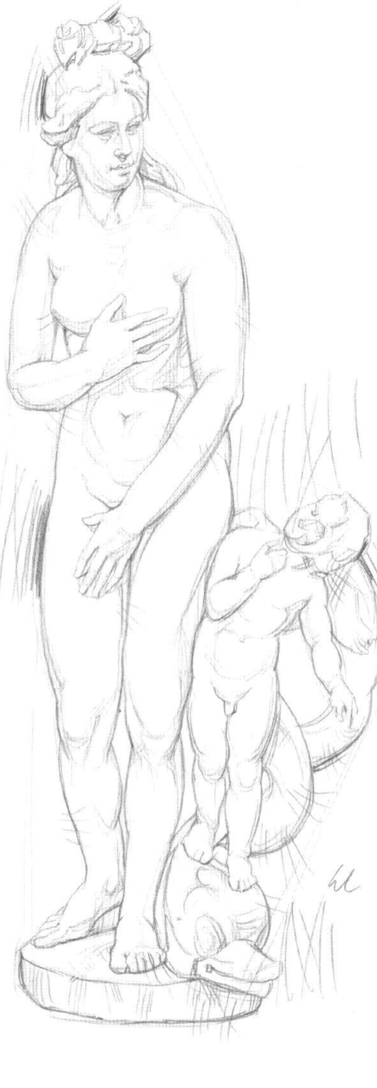

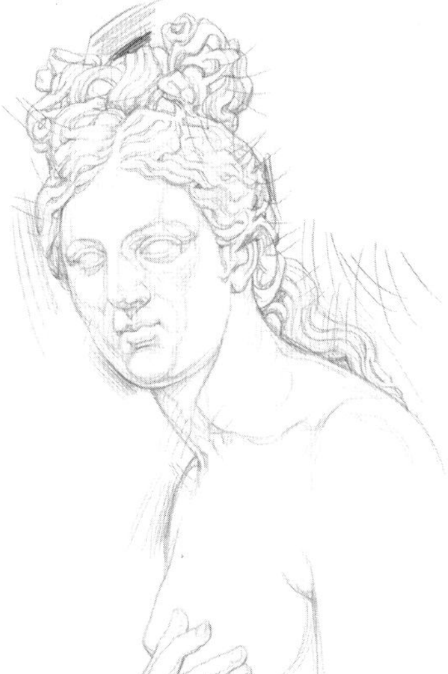

a

The hair is styled in a rather sophisticated fashion (a). For an effective study, only the main volume needs to be drawn, after observing it carefully and analysing the most significant shapes, rather than trying to copy the tiniest, superfluous details.

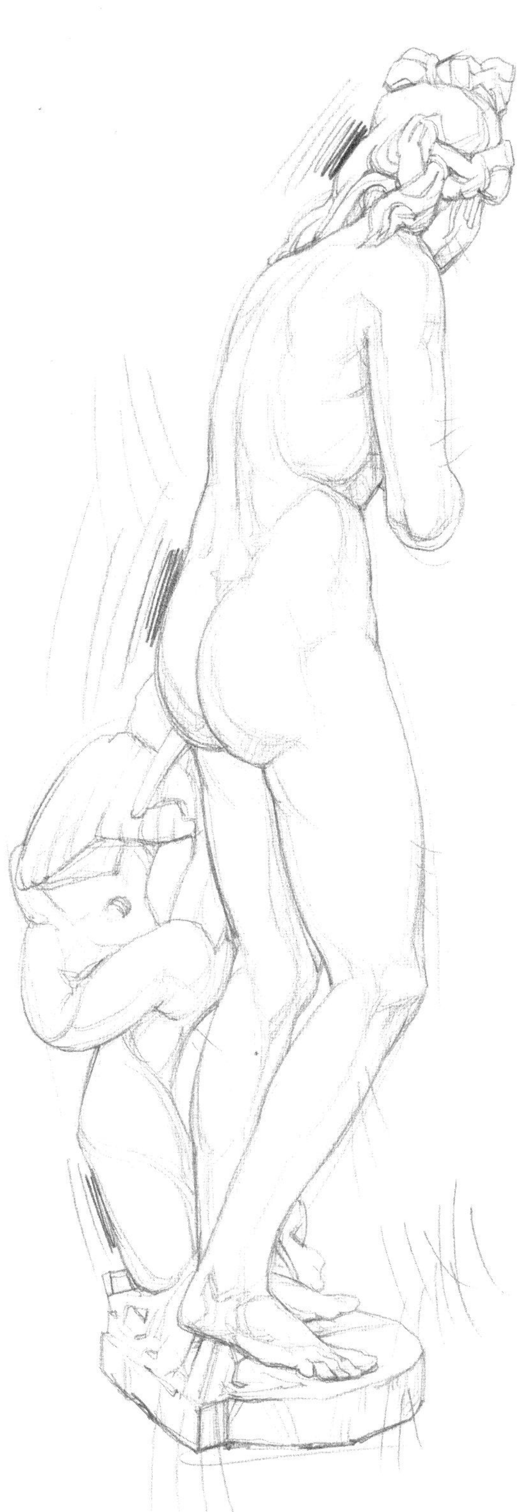

The line of the nose ridge continues and meets the forehead without any angular elements. This is a stylistic characteristic decreeing a high standard of beauty, harmony and rarity although (or maybe because of this) it is not often found in nature.

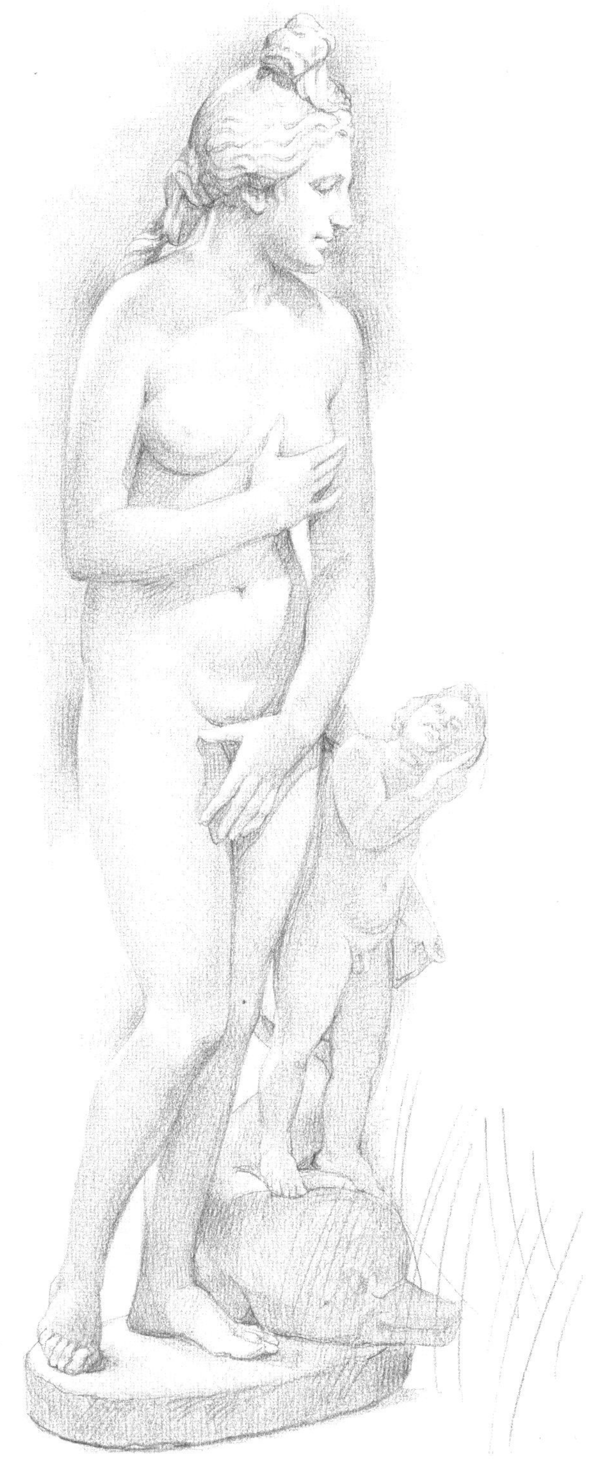

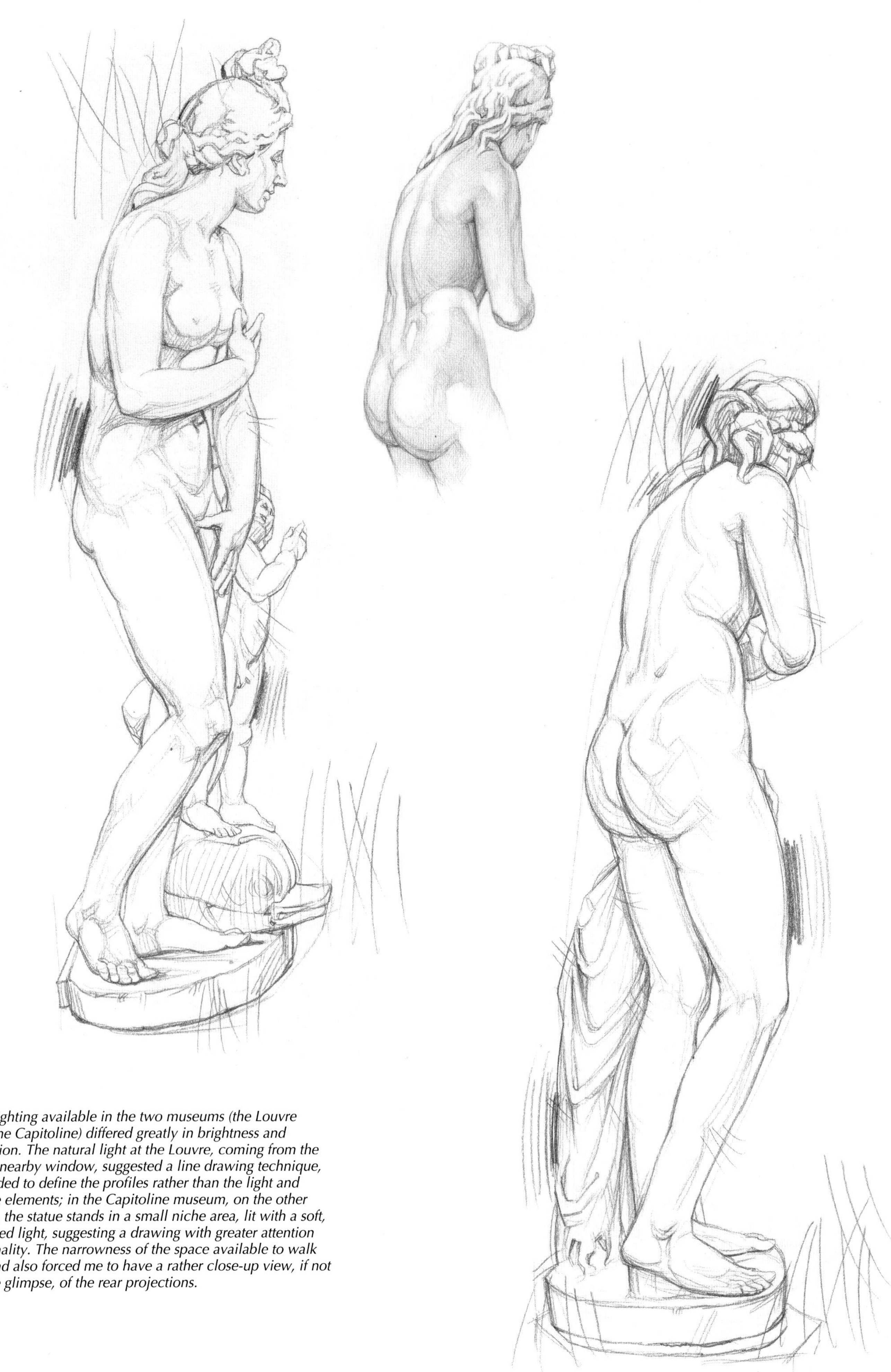

The lighting available in the two museums (the Louvre and the Capitoline) differed greatly in brightness and diffusion. The natural light at the Louvre, coming from the large nearby window, suggested a line drawing technique, intended to define the profiles rather than the light and shade elements; in the Capitoline museum, on the other hand, the statue stands in a small niche area, lit with a soft, diffused light, suggesting a drawing with greater attention to tonality. The narrowness of the space available to walk around also forced me to have a rather close-up view, if not a true glimpse, of the rear projections.

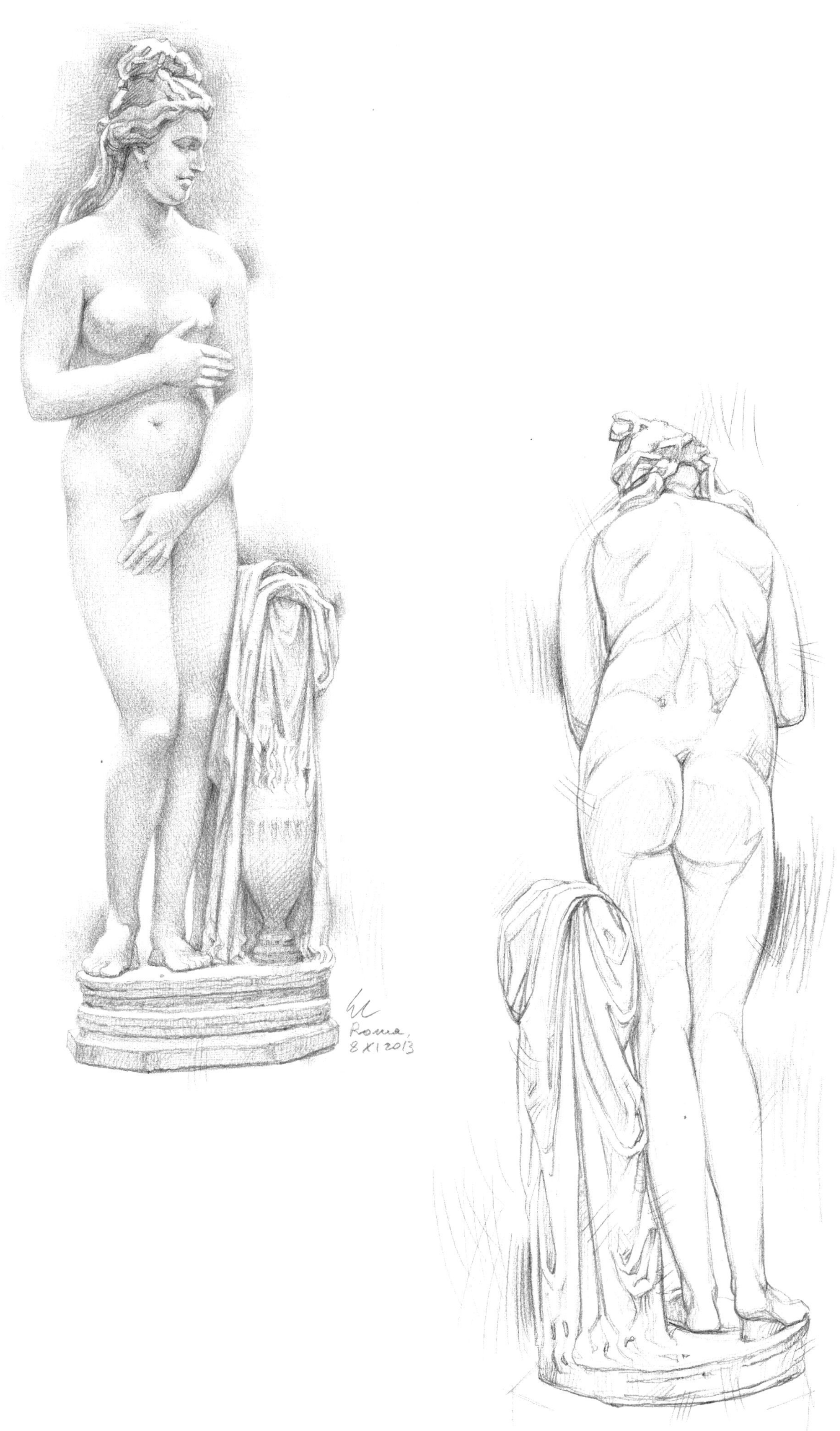
Roma,
8 XI 2013

BELVEDERE TORSO

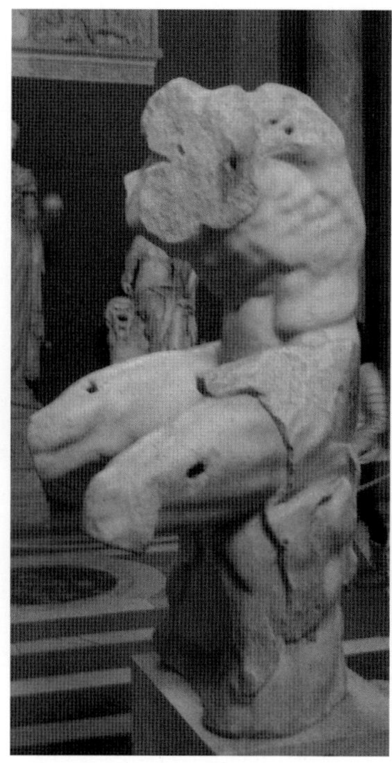

Apollonios of Athens (1st century BC), Torso, *Greek original in marble (circa 50 BC), height 160cm (63in) approximately. Rome, Vatican Museums.*

This sculpture is an original marble fragment from the Late Hellenistic age and is part of an ancient work uncovered in Rome towards the end of the 15th century (the Belvedere was a terraced courtyard in the Vatican). It was almost certainly studied by several artists and also by Michelangelo. Echoes of the forms of this torso can, for example, be seen in the *Day* sculpture in the Medici Chapels or in the *Slaves* statues at the Accademia Gallery in Florence. The identification with Hercules is uncertain, as the residual attributes (feline skin etc.) do not correspond to the actual iconography, and the overall stance seems to be similar to that of the *Boxer at Rest,* a work of art in bronze by the same Greek sculptor.

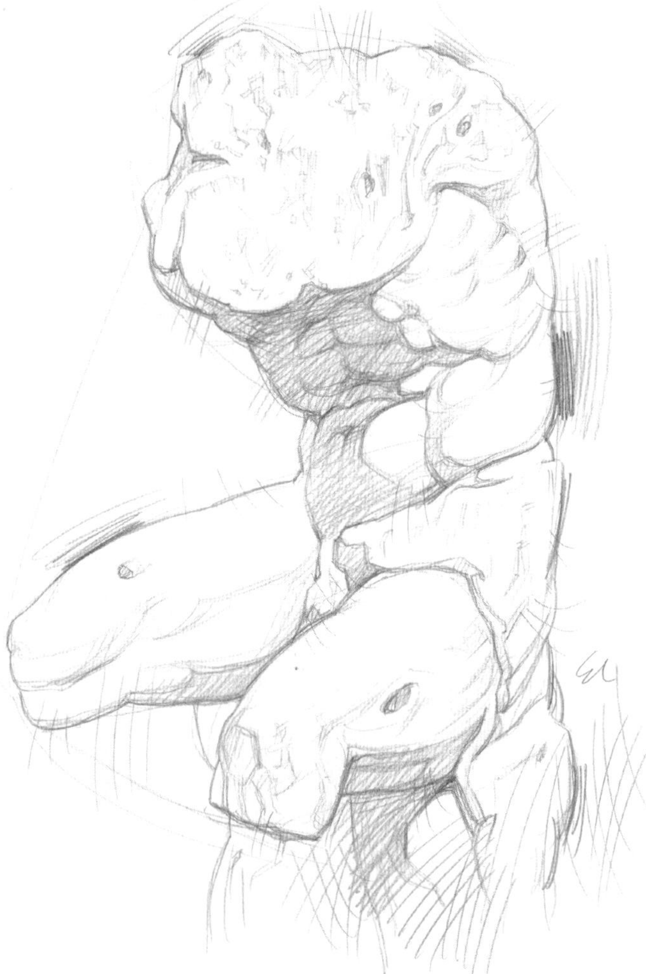

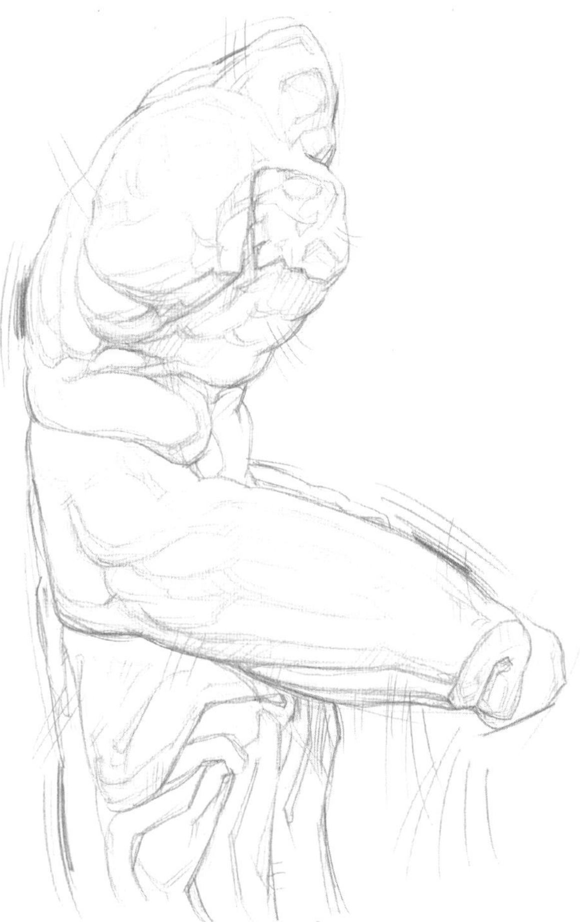

Looking at the anatomic forms only allows a partial theory to be formed about the entire body's posture, which looks powerful, but of which only the torso and thighs remain. The body is slightly bent forwards (in order to adapt to the contracting abdominal muscles and show clear folds in the skin) and just slightly turned to his left. This places his shoulders at different levels: the right one lower than the other, which may have been attached to an arm that was raised and separated from the body, which would justify the breadth of the residual underarm cavity. The right arm could have been in a closer position to the torso, almost resting on the right thigh.

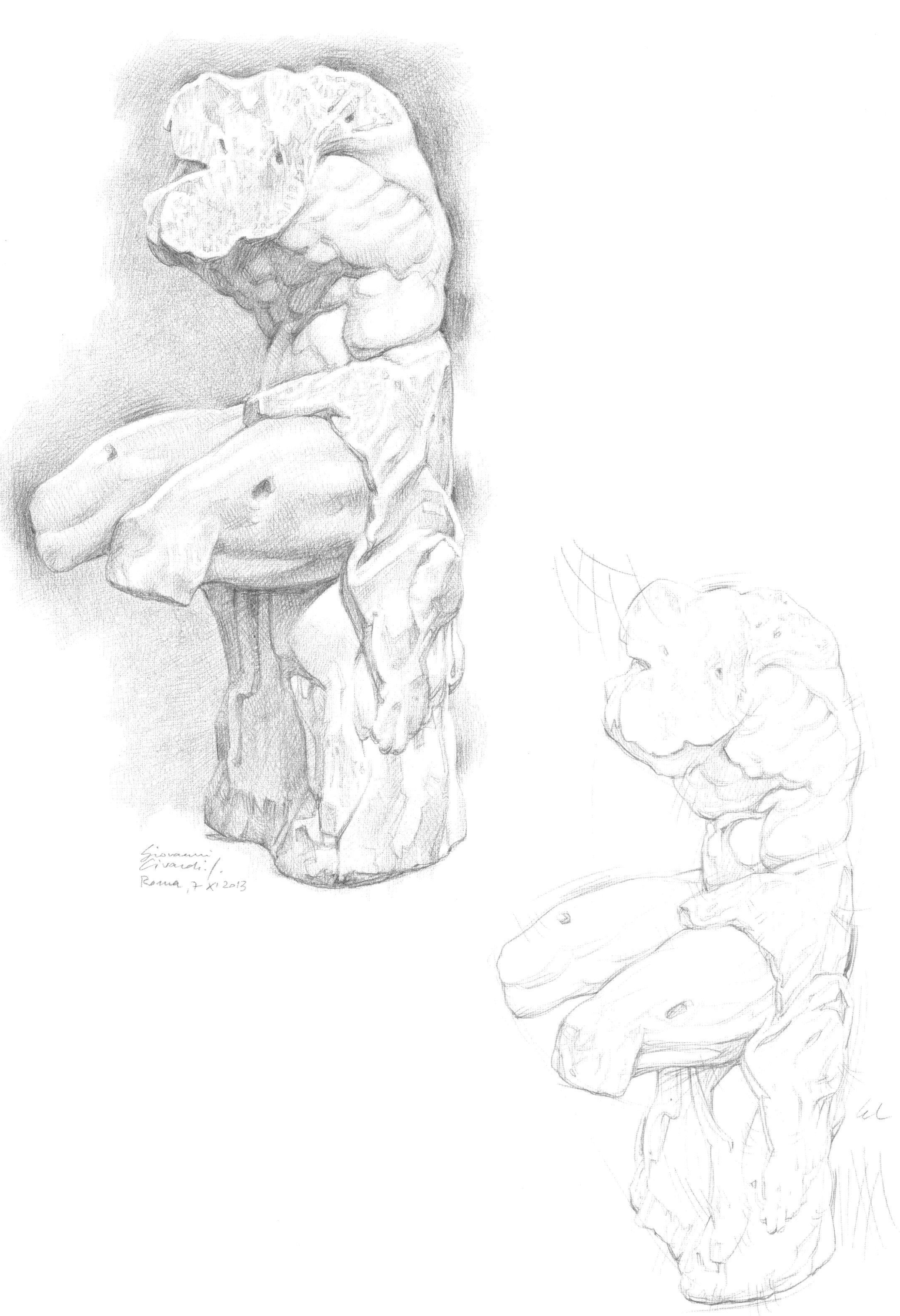
Giovanni Civardi f.
Roma, 7 XI 2013

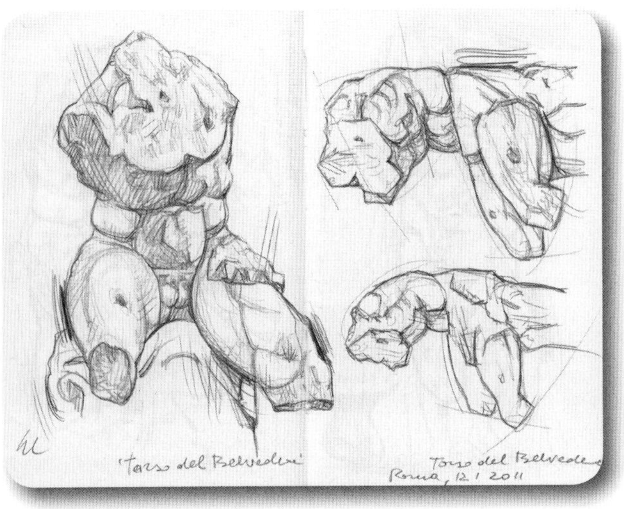

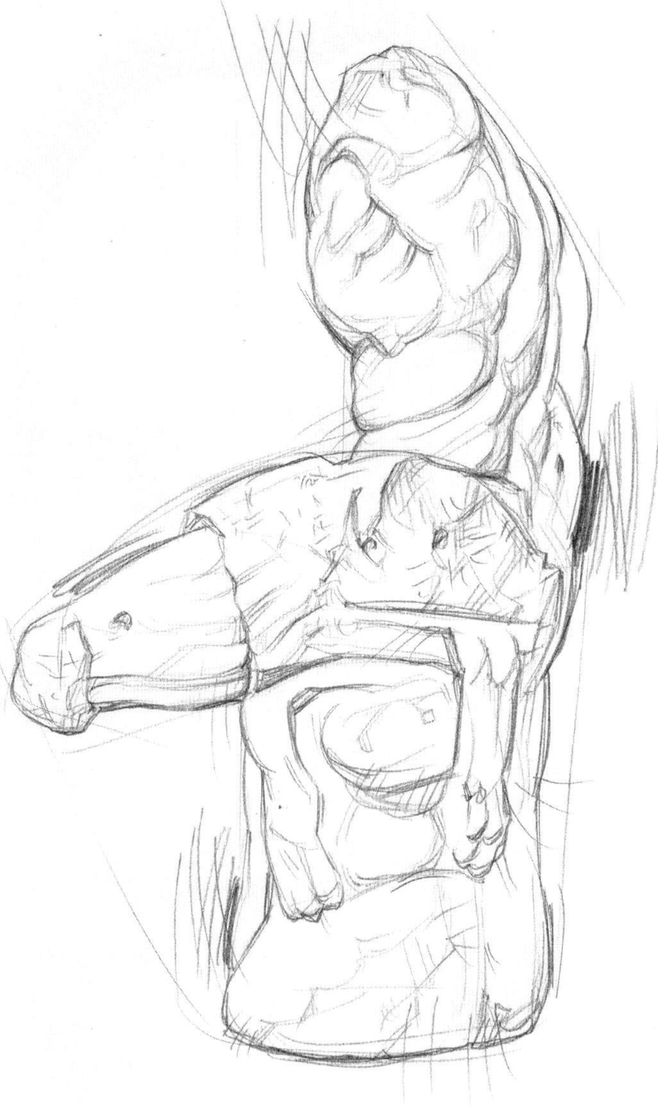

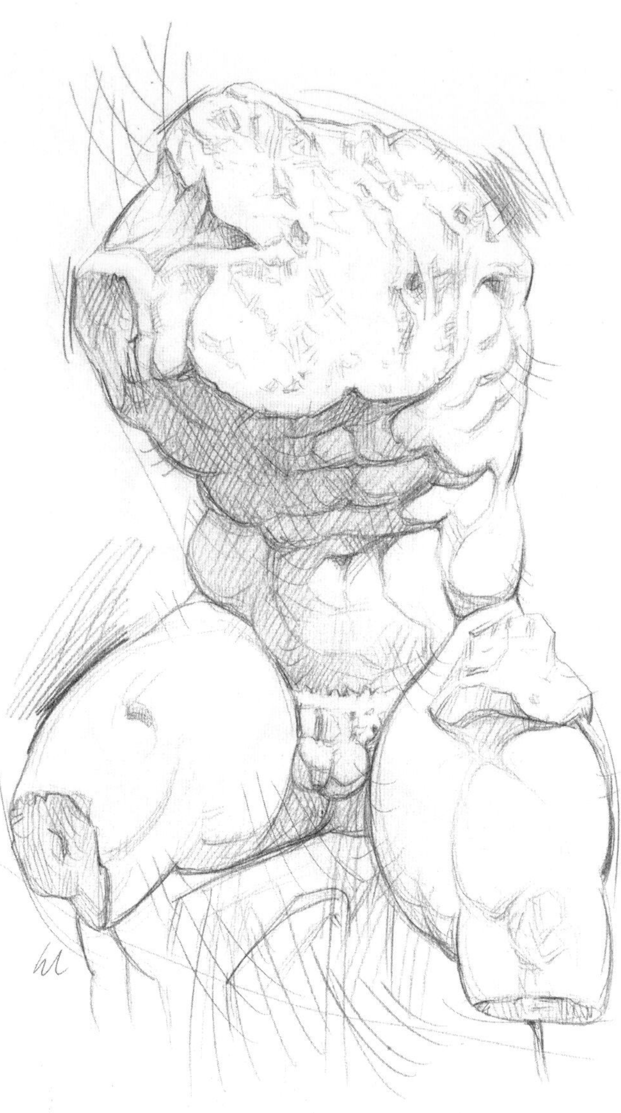

The size of the muscles in the thighs and the slight hint of contraction suggest that the right leg was partly bent, so that the foot would be close to the rock on which the figure is sitting. The lowered position and the clear raised nature of the parts of the left knee (kneecap, tendon, etc.) lead us to imagine that the left leg was stretched out quite far forwards.

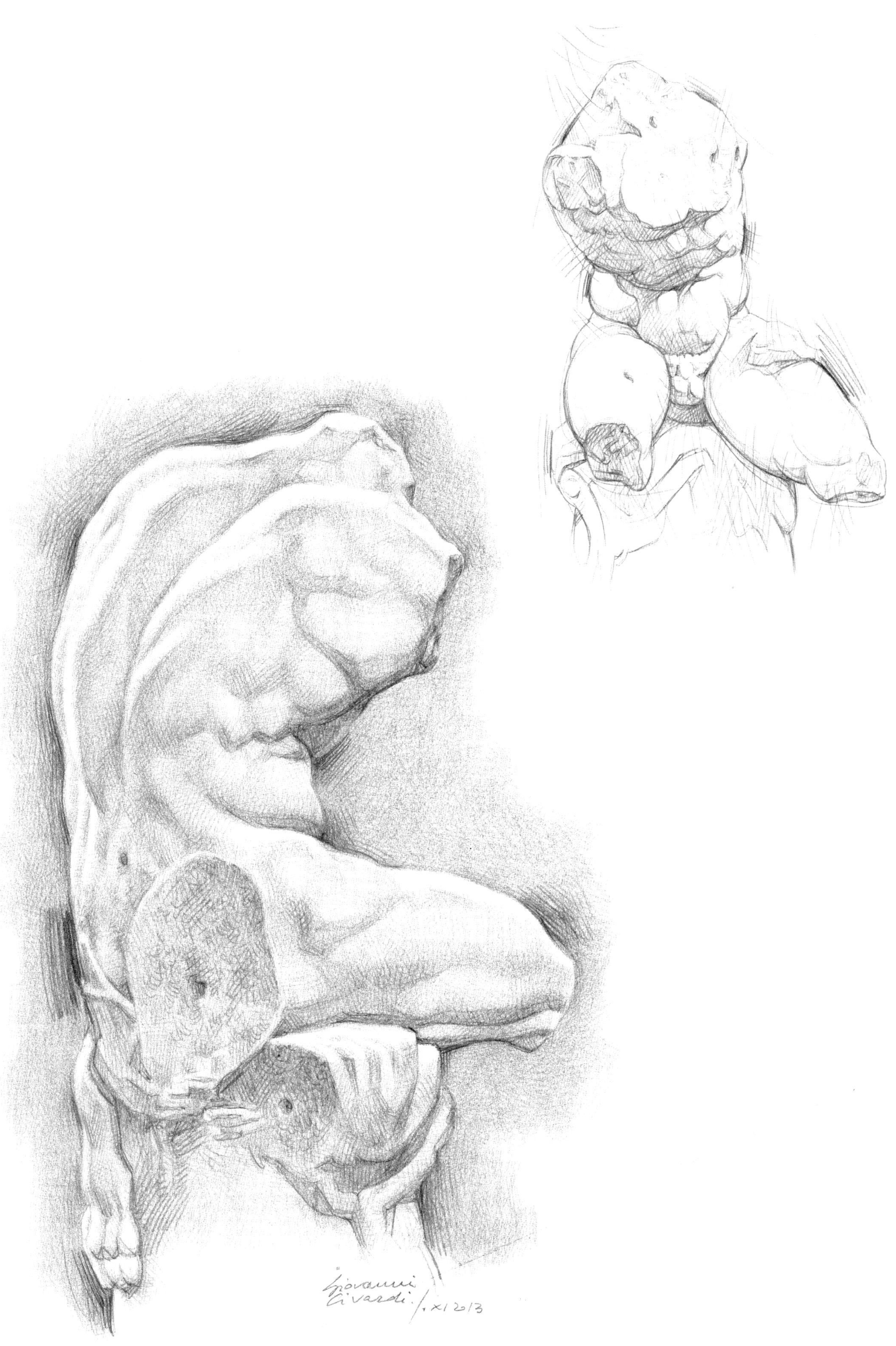
Giovanni
Civardi. / . XI 2013

VENUS DE MILO

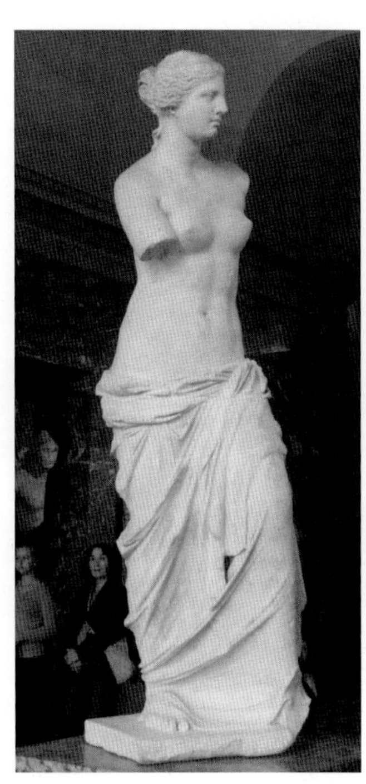

Aphrodite de Milo, *better known as* Venus de Milo, *Greek original in marble (circa 100 BC), height 202cm (79½in). Paris, Musée du Louvre.*

This is one of the most famous ancient sculptures: it is set apart in a large, well-lit room at the Louvre and in spite of the large number of people that crowd around it, it is quite easy to observe and draw, taking your time and looking at the sculpture from different points of view and distances. The goddess only appears to have a naked upper body, while the lower part is covered by a draped cloth. this is held at the height of the hips and is bundled into close folds around her left leg, which is bent and raised as it rests on a small mound on the ground. The stance is one of *contrapposto* or counterpose; the weight of the body rests on the right leg and the left leg helps to keep the balance. The cross axis of her shoulders tilts in the opposite direction to that of her pelvis and is also slightly twisted, giving the figure an almost spiral pose that wraps the body around itself vertically. Unlike the classic chiastic pose, however, the head is turned to the side of the bent limb and not towards the supporting limb.

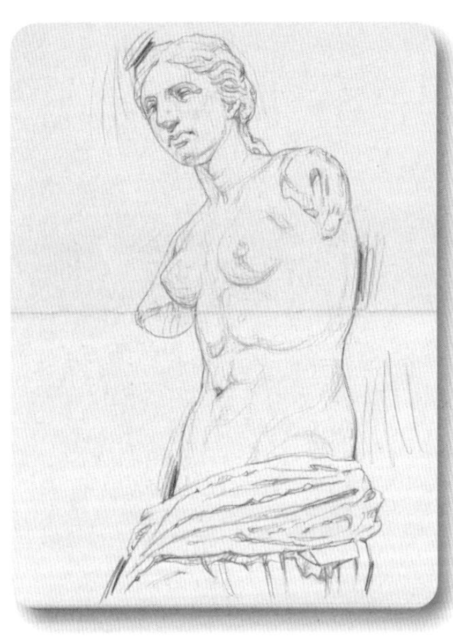

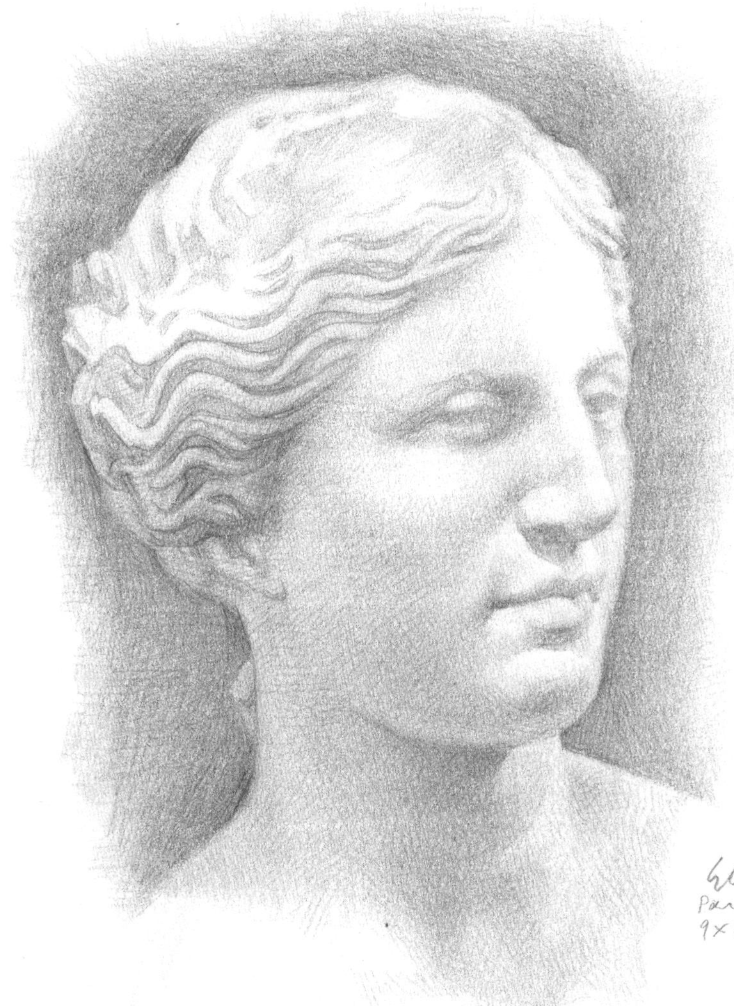

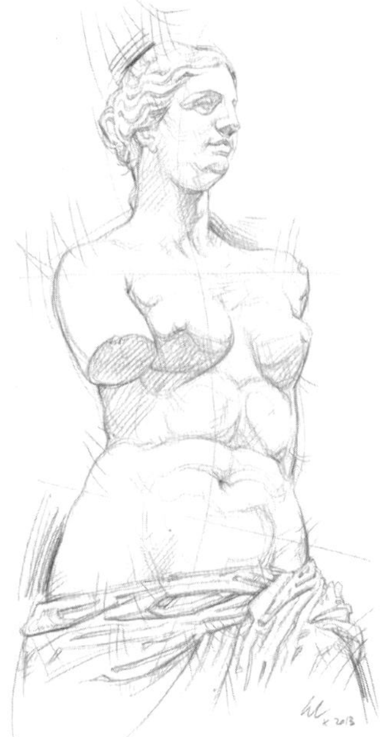

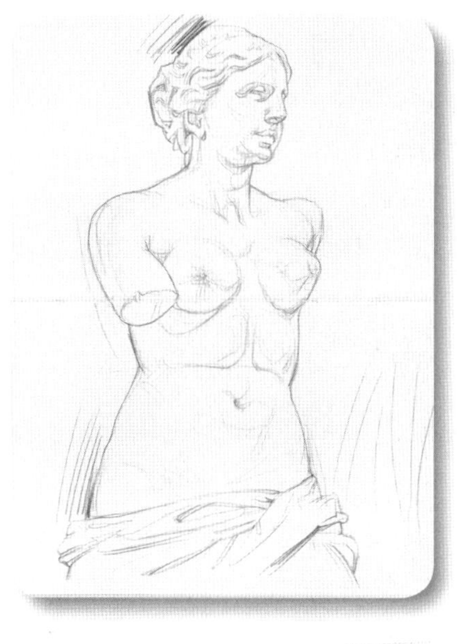

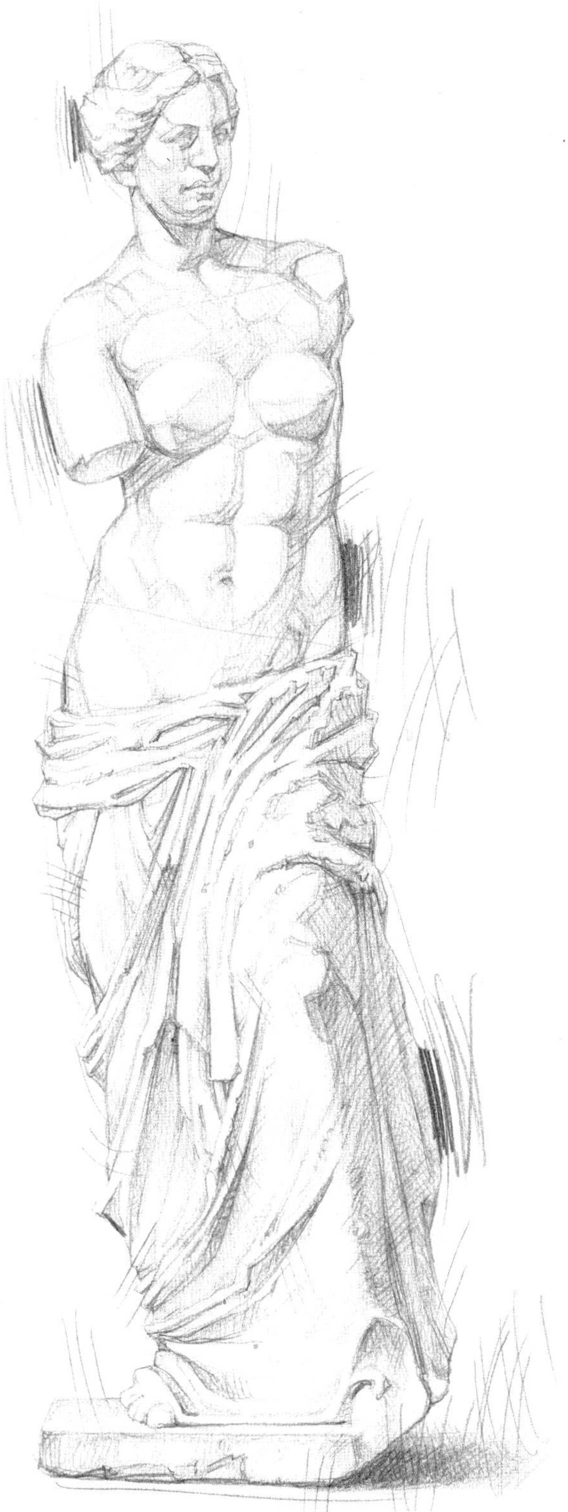

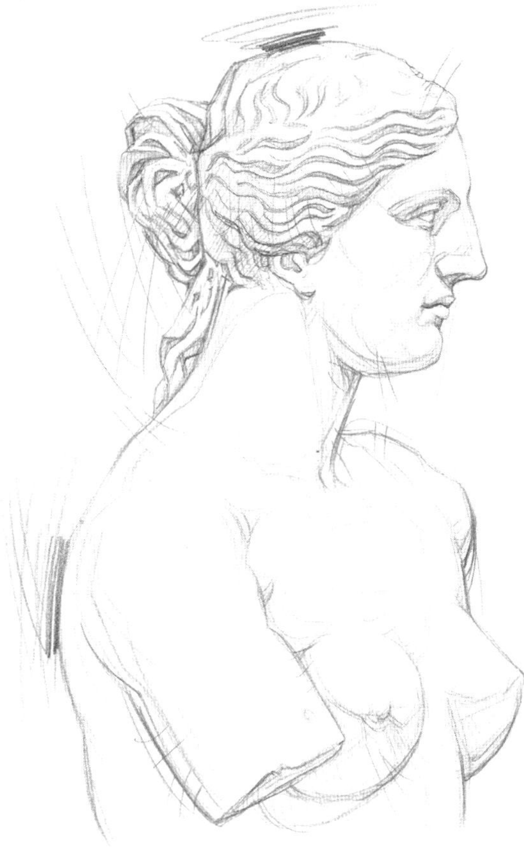

The spiral structure can be seen better in a slightly side view; in a frontal view, on the other hand, in addition to seeing the direction of the contrapposto, it is easier to see the different profile of the two sides of the torso (extended and stretched on the left, contracted on the right) and a number of oblique lines that should ideally run along the axis of the main segments. For example, the torso axis (especially at the height of the abdomen) tilts in the opposite direction to the axis of the head, the chest and the supporting limb, which are also parallel to each other.

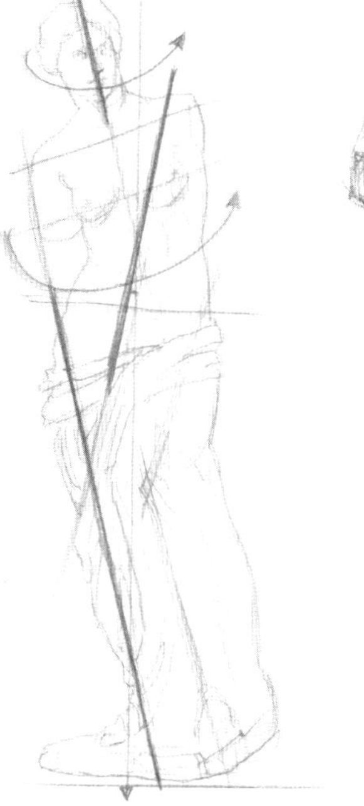

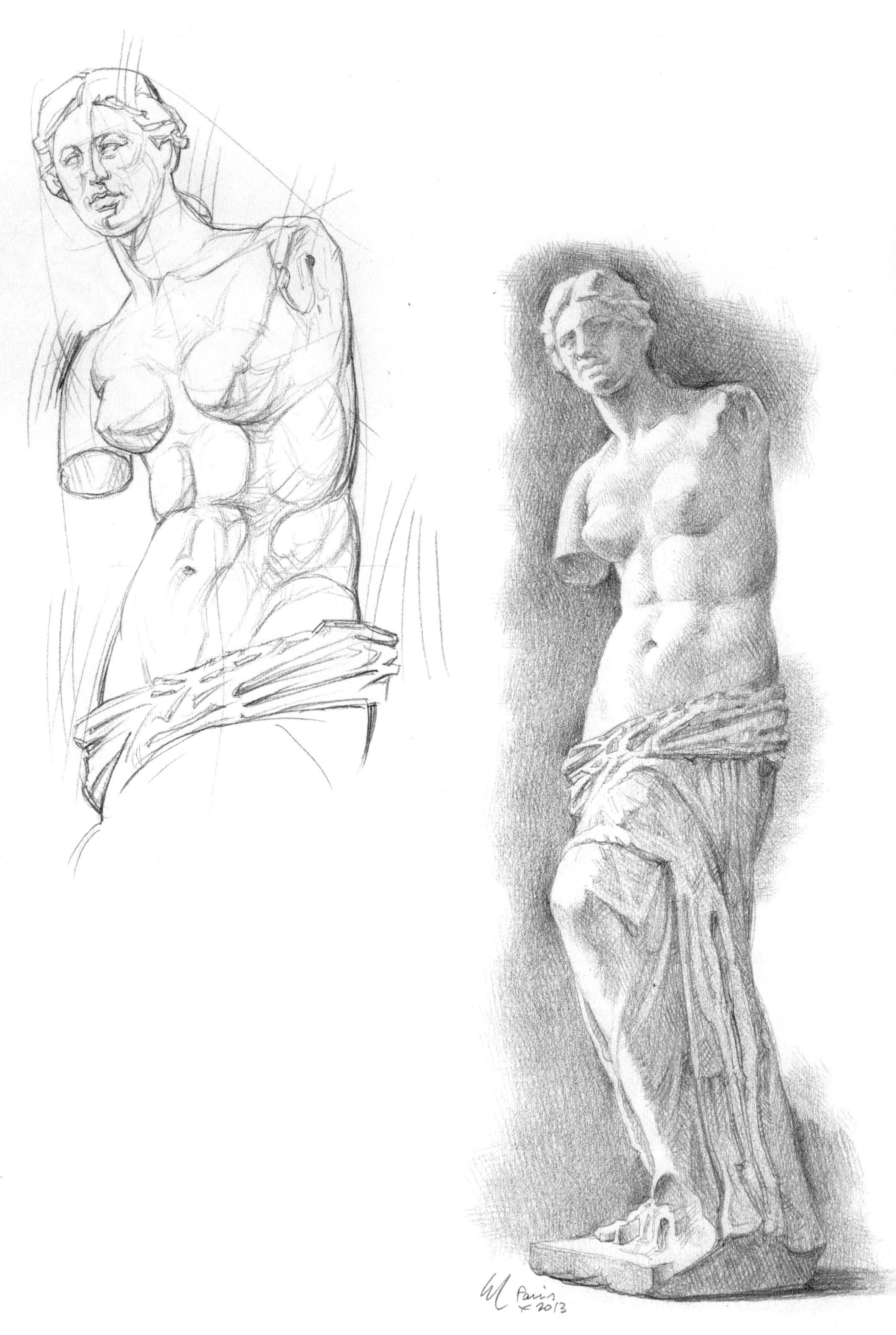
Paris
X 2013

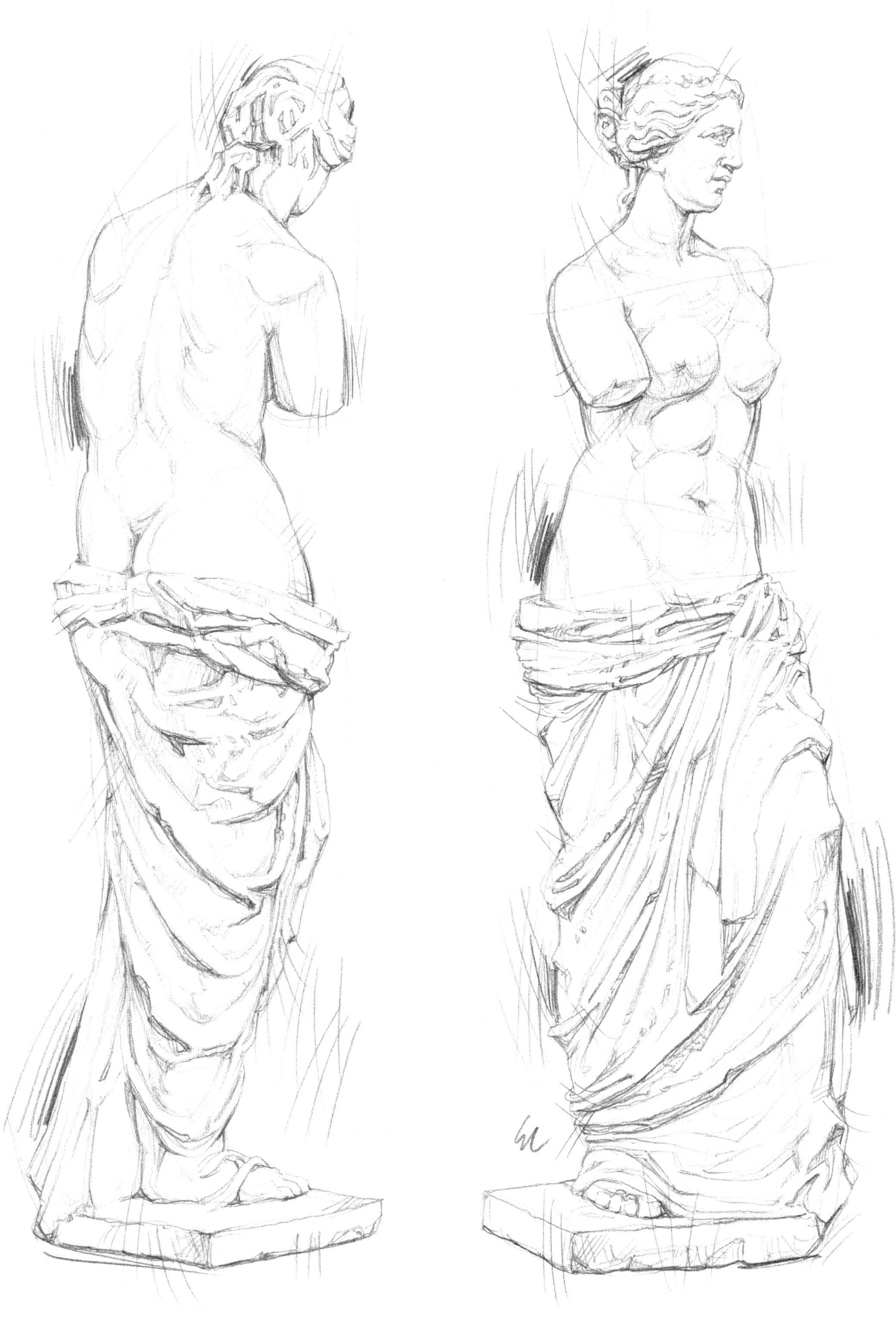

MOSES

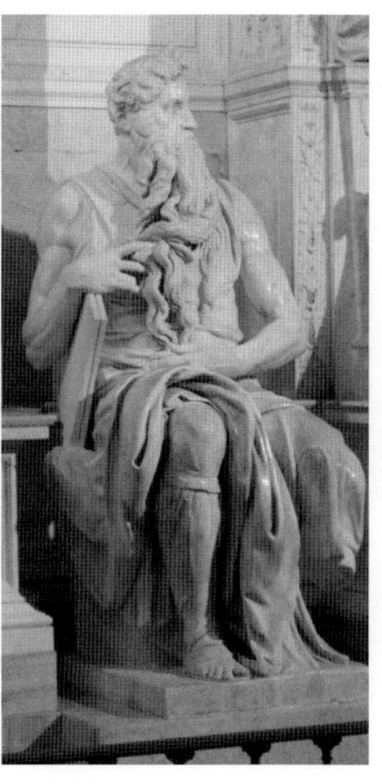

Michelangelo Buonarroti (1475–1564), Moses *(circa 1515), marble, height 235cm (92¾in). Rome, San Pietro in Vincoli (Tomb of Julius II).*

The Tomb of Pope Julius II provided Michelangelo with the opportunity to create some of his masterpieces: *Moses* and *Slaves*. *Moses* can be drawn taking your time, as it is housed in a church and, except for the times when religious services are held, you can stand just a few metres from the statue to draw it from various front and side views. The ordinary lighting is diffused and sufficient but artificial lighting, which is more concentrated and intense, is switched on all too often, with the intention of highlighting the play of light and shade for visitors. In the original project for the tomb, this statue was planned for an elevated position and, therefore, for being viewed from below. This accounts for the changes made to perspective, several times, by Michelangelo, to correct the optical effects through proportional devices: lengthening the torso, enlarging the head, accentuating the right leg and the cloak lying on top of it, etc.

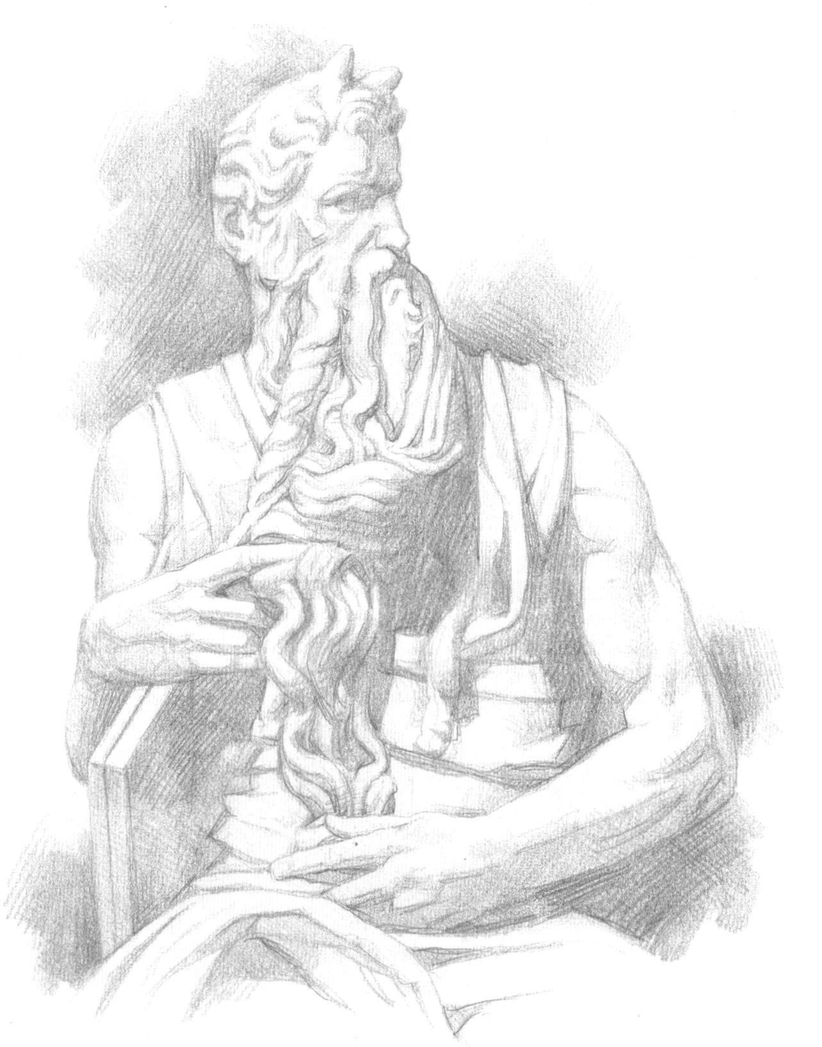

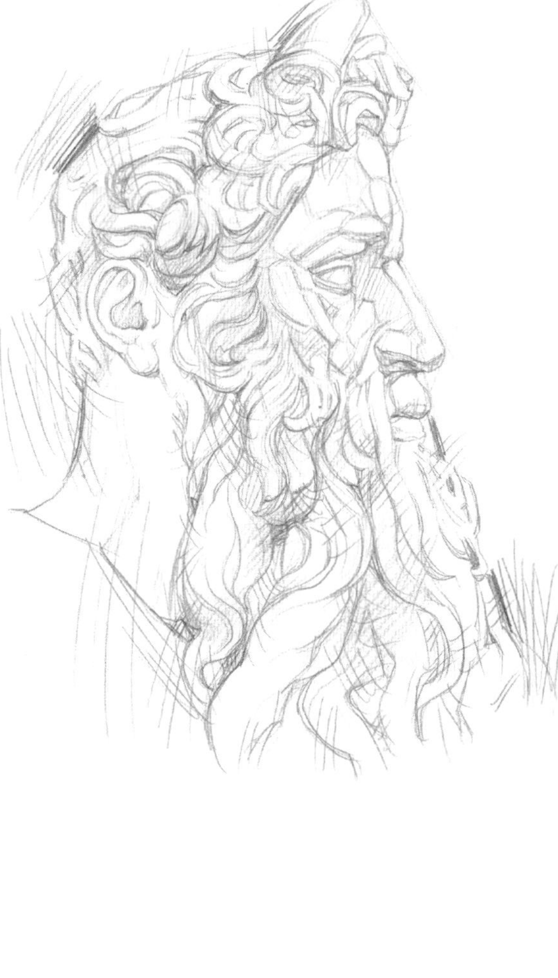

Two horns emerge from the figure's hair on his forehead, the fine streaks of which suggest and symbolise rays of divine light coming from the prophet when he came down from Mount Sinai.

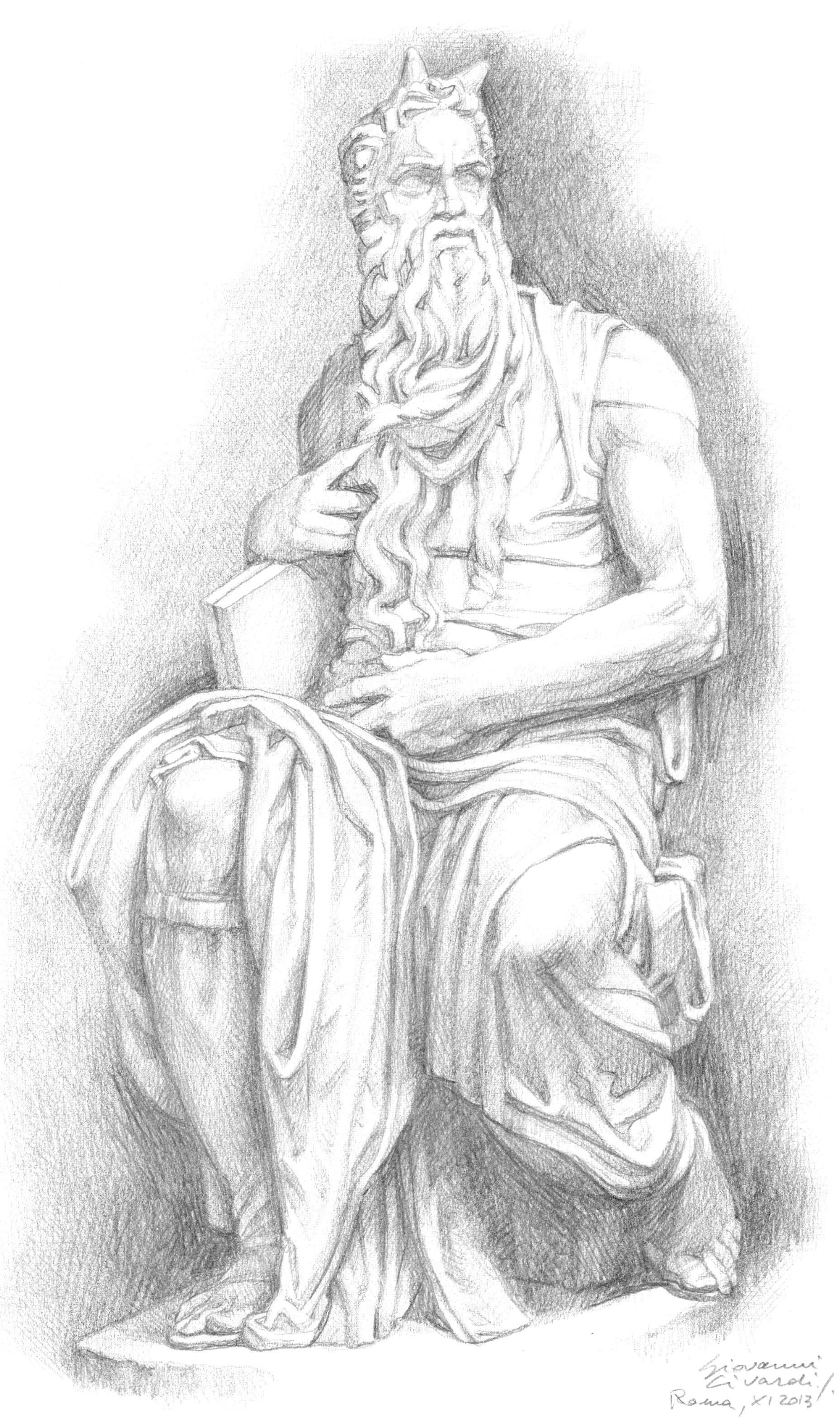
Giovanni Civardi
Roma, XI 2013

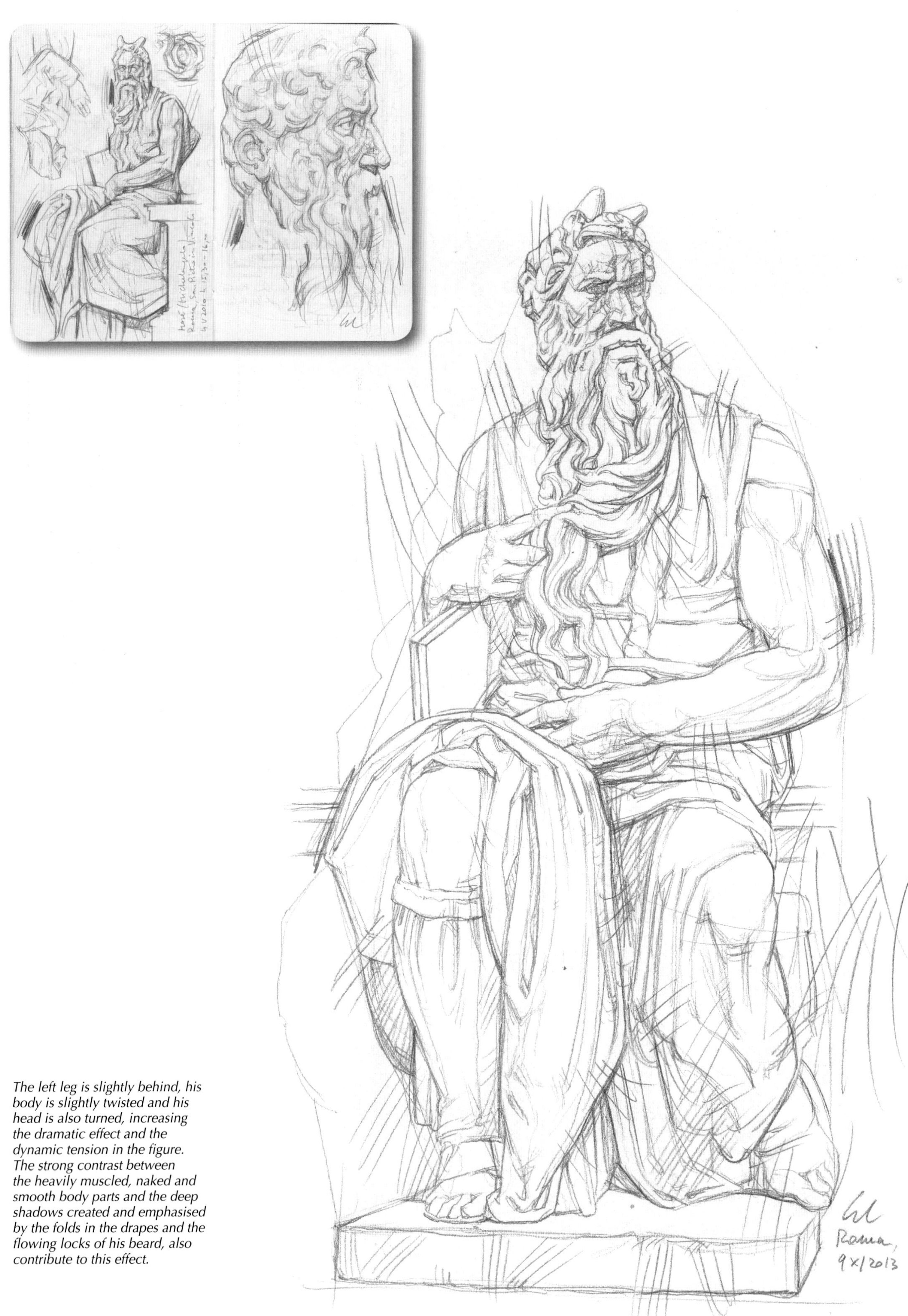

The left leg is slightly behind, his body is slightly twisted and his head is also turned, increasing the dramatic effect and the dynamic tension in the figure. The strong contrast between the heavily muscled, naked and smooth body parts and the deep shadows created and emphasised by the folds in the drapes and the flowing locks of his beard, also contribute to this effect.

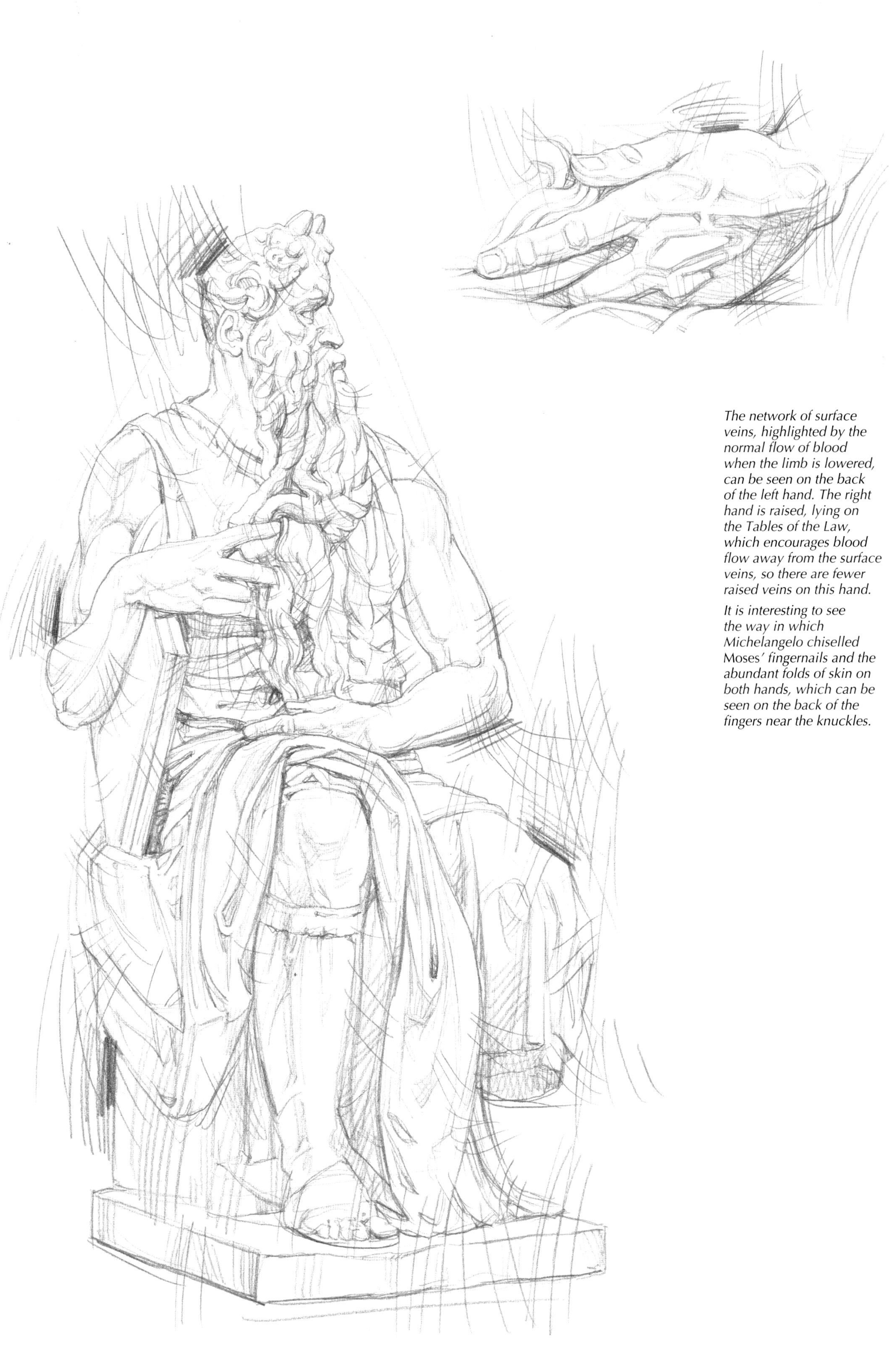

The network of surface veins, highlighted by the normal flow of blood when the limb is lowered, can be seen on the back of the left hand. The right hand is raised, lying on the Tables of the Law, which encourages blood flow away from the surface veins, so there are fewer raised veins on this hand.

It is interesting to see the way in which Michelangelo chiselled Moses' fingernails and the abundant folds of skin on both hands, which can be seen on the back of the fingers near the knuckles.

DYING SLAVE

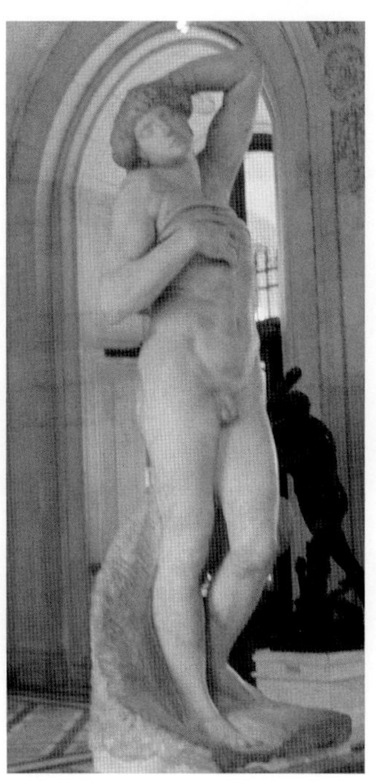

Michelangelo Buonarroti (1475–1564), Dying Slave *(circa 1513–1516), Carrara marble, height 229cm (90½in). Paris, Musée du Louvre.*

The *Slaves* were sculpted by Michelangelo as part of his project for the tomb of Pope Julius II. The favoured frontal pose of both slaves and the rough sculpting of the bases and the rears of the bodies lead us to assume that the statues were to be placed in the monument's niches or corners. The *Dying Slave* strikes a pose of abandon: languorous, bending and almost symbolic of the extreme moment that lies between forced restraint and free expansion into an existential experience, the moment between mortal lethargy and reawakening. A small, barely sketched-out monkey is placed next to the slave's left leg, almost alluding to the mimicry of the arts and knowledge.

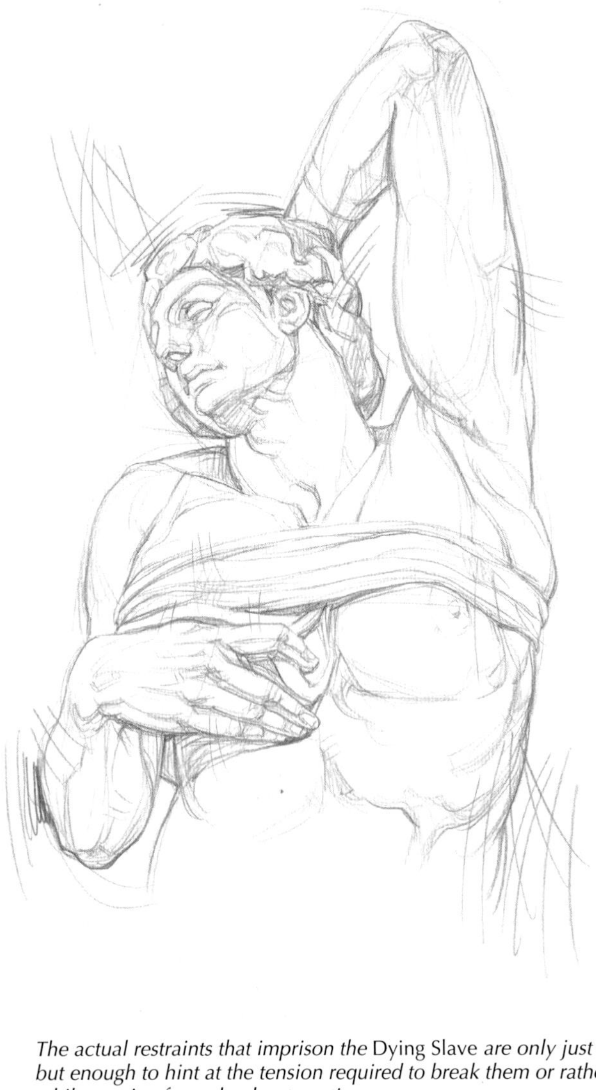

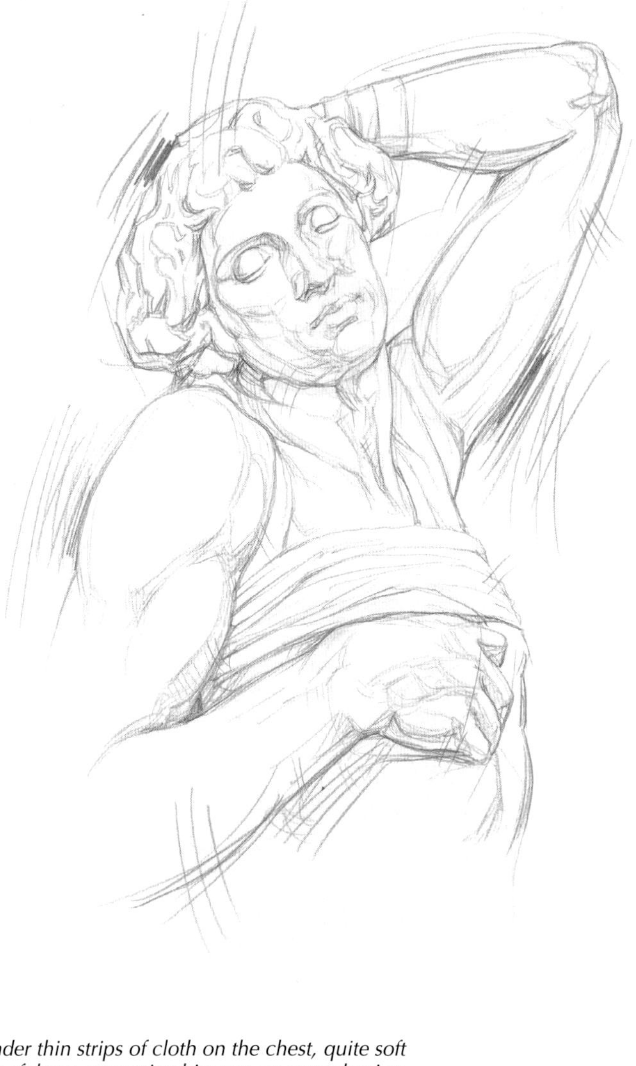

The actual restraints that imprison the Dying Slave *are only just visible under thin strips of cloth on the chest, quite soft but enough to hint at the tension required to break them or rather slip out of them, reopening his eyes on reawakening while moving from slumber to action.*

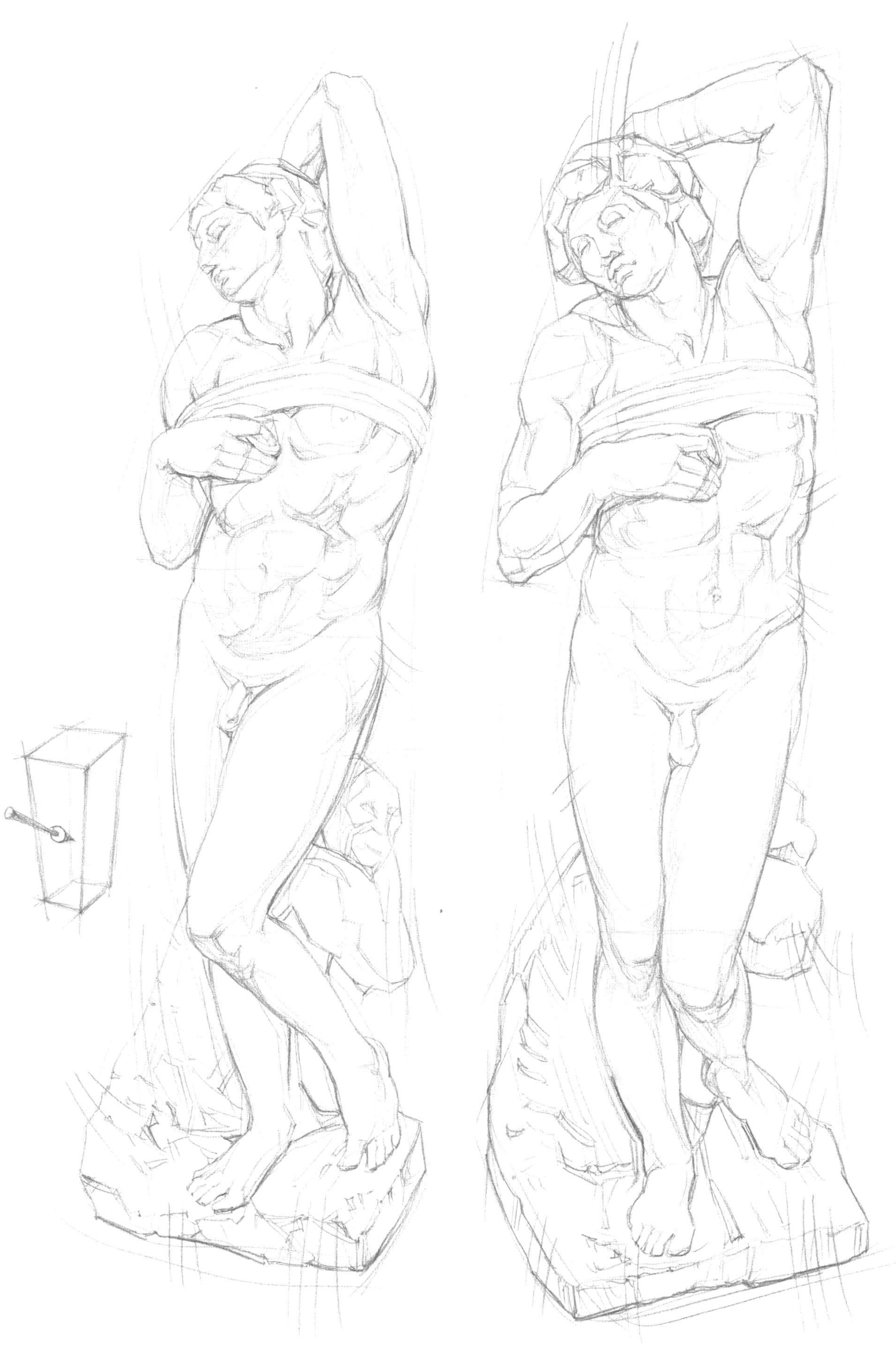

The two drawings shown on this page do not refer to the original sculpture (the one in the Louvre), but are taken from identical plaster copies kept at the Picasso Museum in Antibes. They stand on the landing of a staircase, allowing me to draw them from an unusual perspective, a view from a slightly higher location.

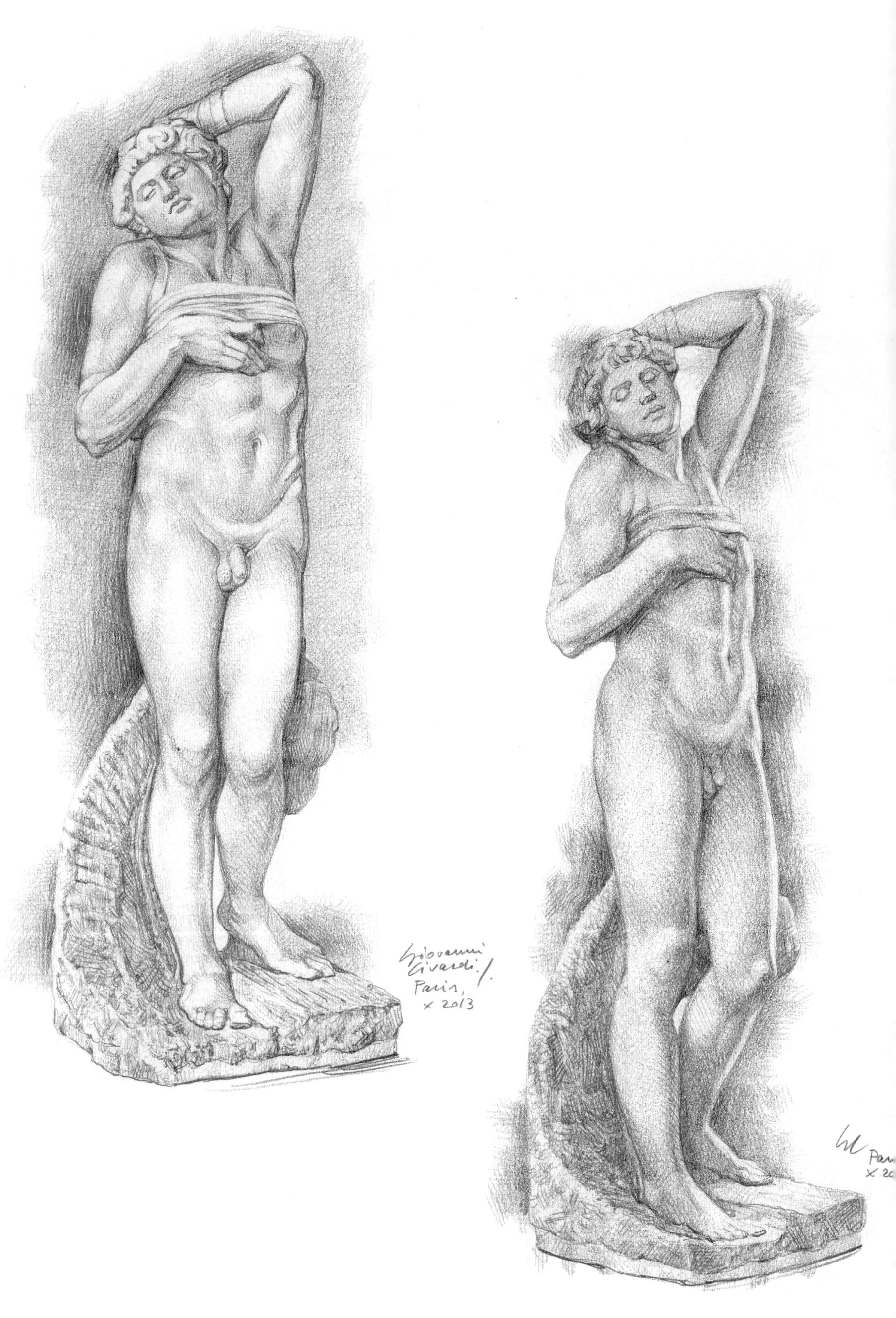
Giovanni Civardi /.
Paris,
x 2013

In addition to aesthetic and emotional considerations, when we observe human figures as portrayed in the best ancient sculptures, it provides us with an opportunity to carry out a brief survey of anatomical structure and the way in which it is interpreted by the artist. Here, for example, I have tried to identify the form, position and ratios in the muscles in the left arm (from the medial position) and in the corresponding underarm cavity.

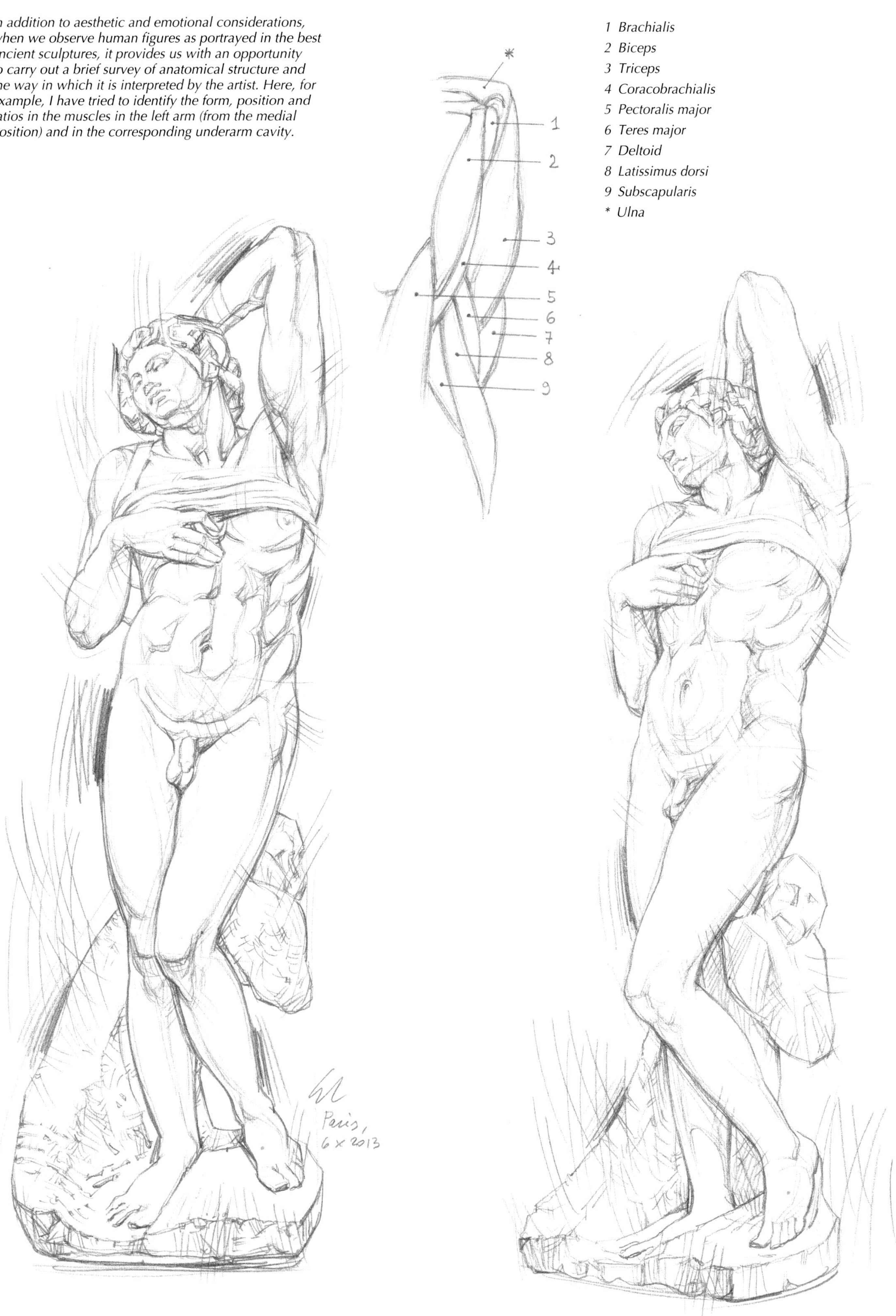

1 Brachialis
2 Biceps
3 Triceps
4 Coracobrachialis
5 Pectoralis major
6 Teres major
7 Deltoid
8 Latissimus dorsi
9 Subscapularis
** Ulna*

REBELLIOUS SLAVE

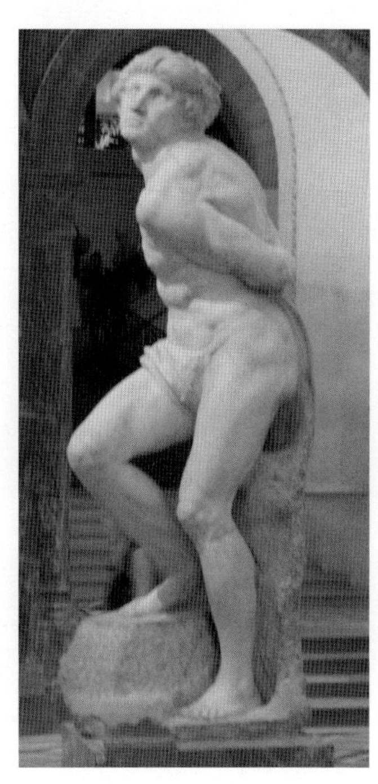

Michelangelo Buonarroti (1475–1564), Rebellious Slave *(circa 1513–1516), Carrara marble, height 209cm (82½in). Paris, Musée du Louvre.*

While the *Dying Slave* strikes a delicately balanced pose of apparent calm serenity while awaiting his reawakening to action, the *Rebellious Slave* is placed in firm contrast, in a tense act of combat. The powerful, contracted muscles show the effort in the arms to release themselves from the restraints that tie them to the body behind the back, while his right leg is bent and quivers in an attempt to free himself of the material that imprisons him, while supporting him at the same time. Perhaps for adaptation to the place where it should have found its final positioning, the sculpture is only fully completed on some sides, especially the ones intended for front viewing or from the left diagonal side, while all the right side is left in a rather rough state of finish.

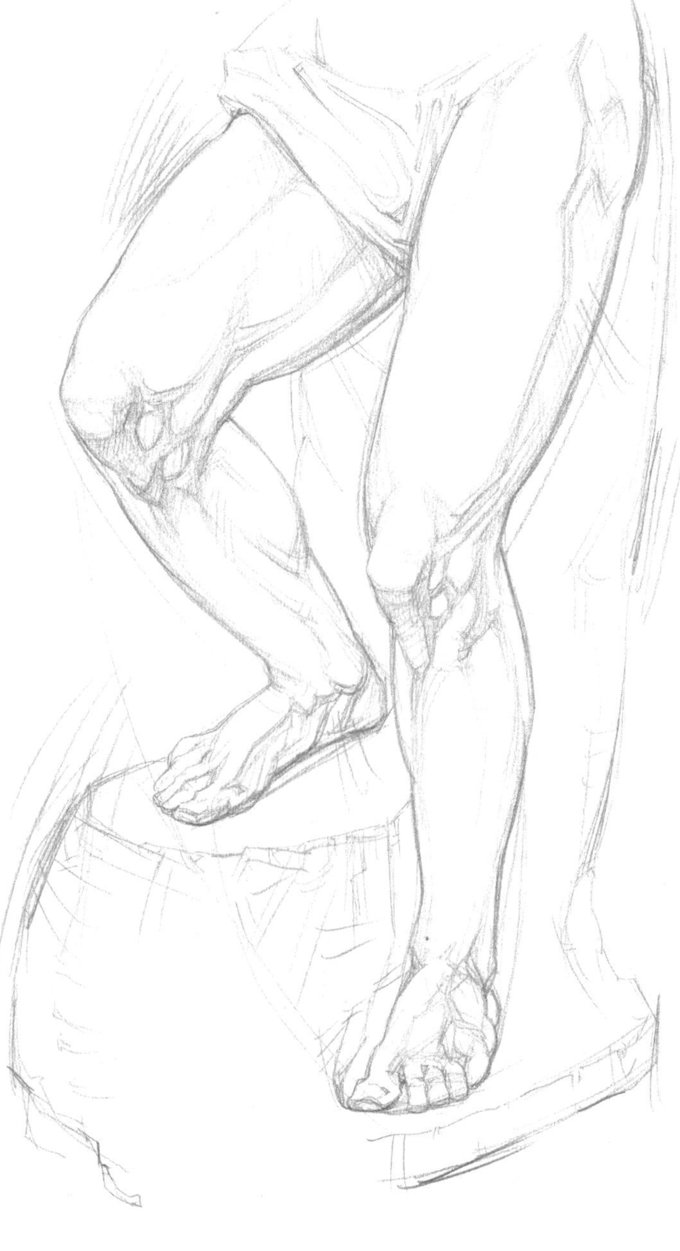

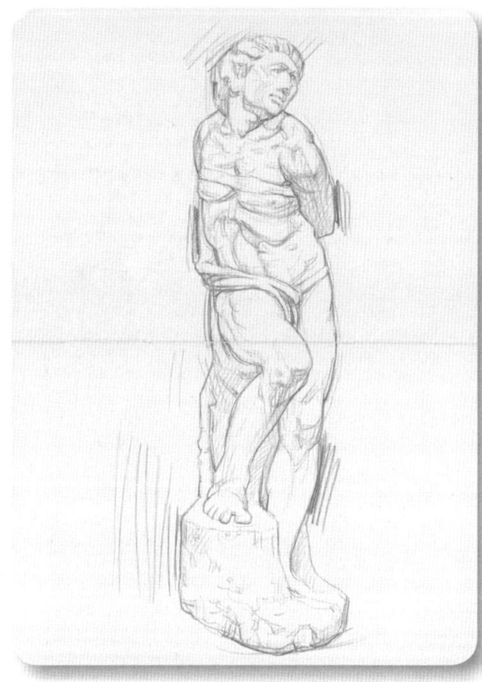

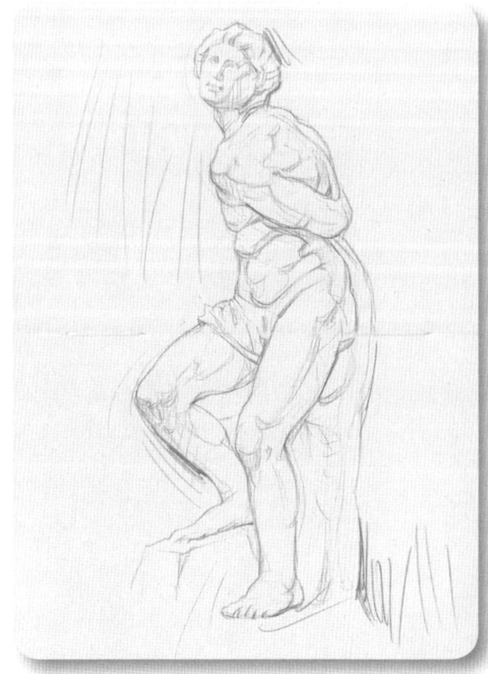

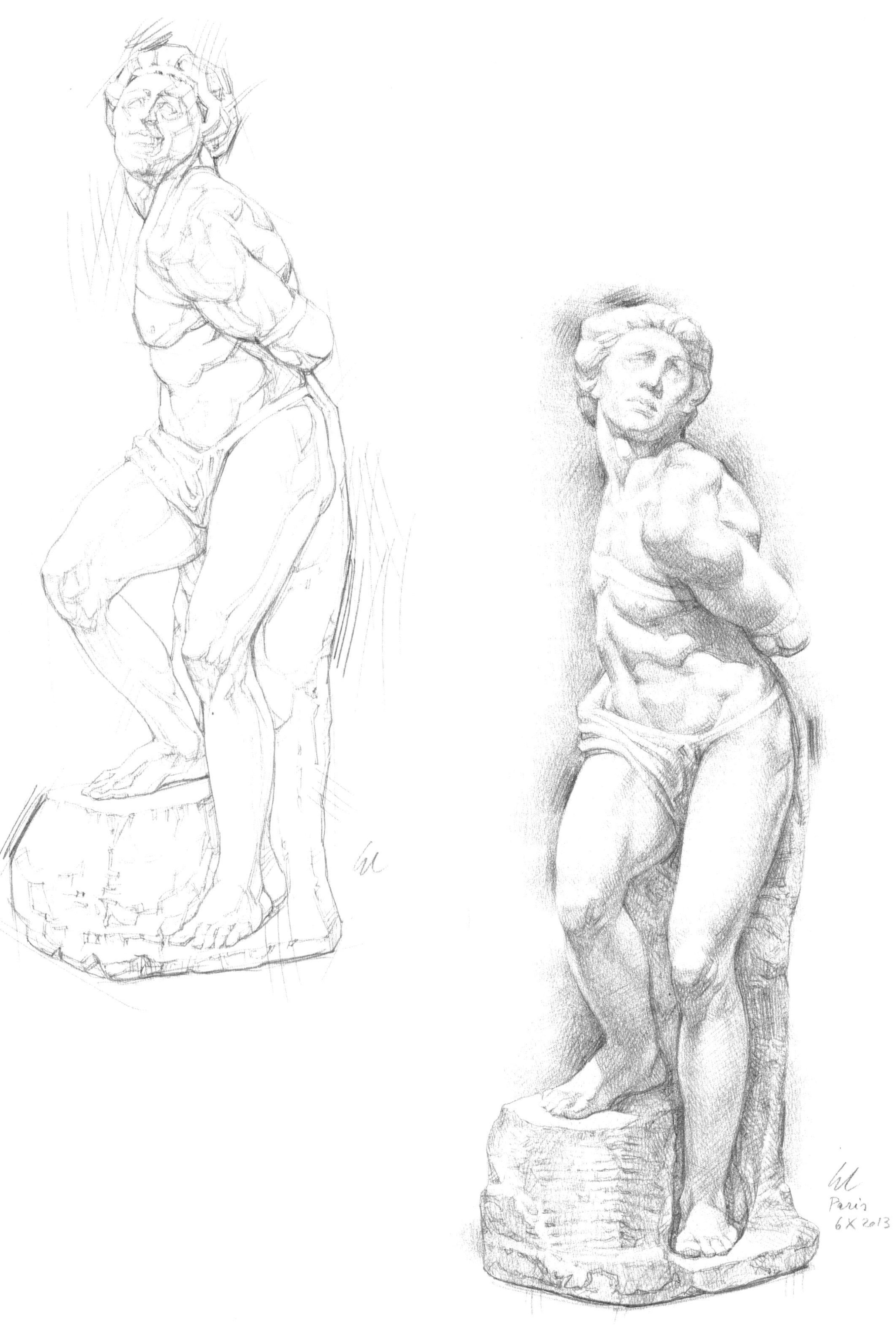
Paris
6 X 2013

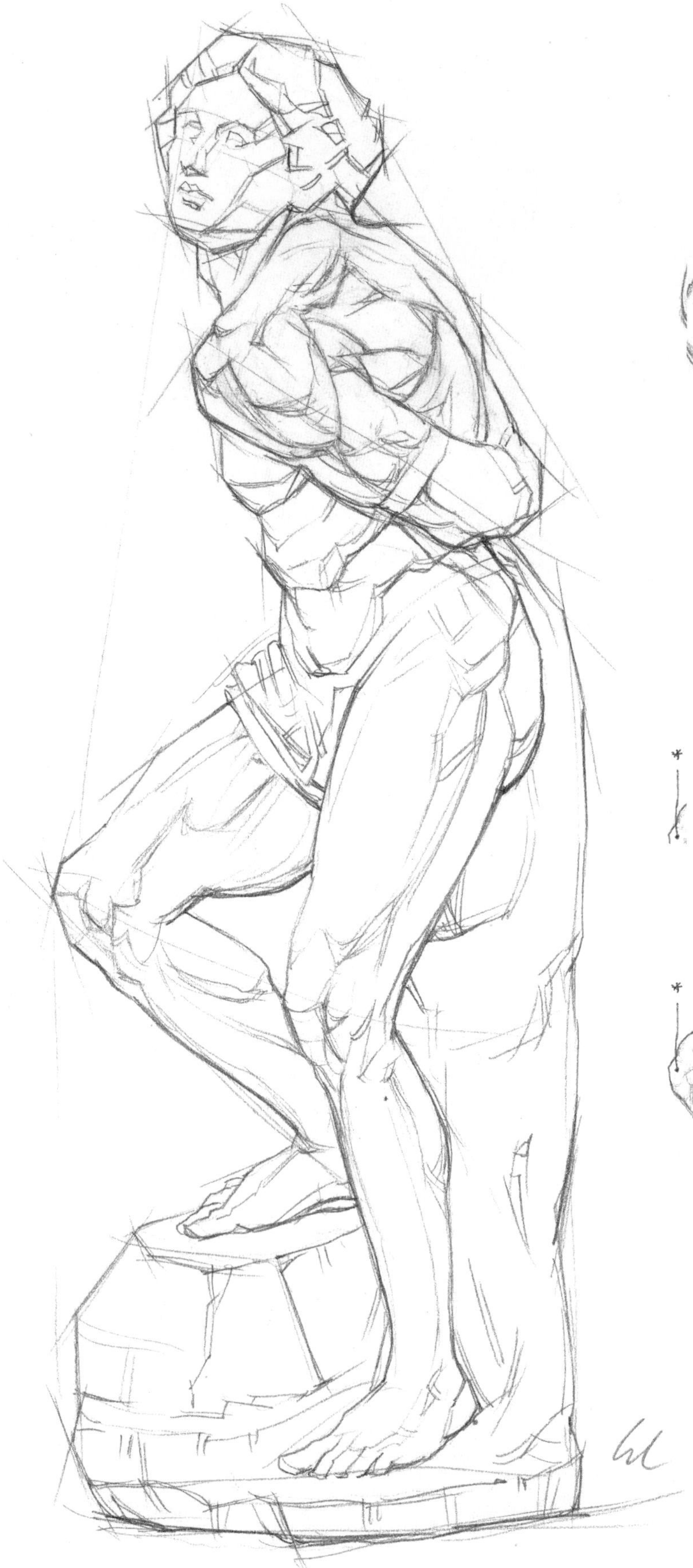

The twisting of the body, the left shoulder brought forward (the right one is only just depicted) and the bent right leg, create harmonies and contrasts and force the muscular contraction and tension in movement to a high level. It may be useful to analyse the muscular structure of the left shoulder and the right thigh, seen from the medial position.

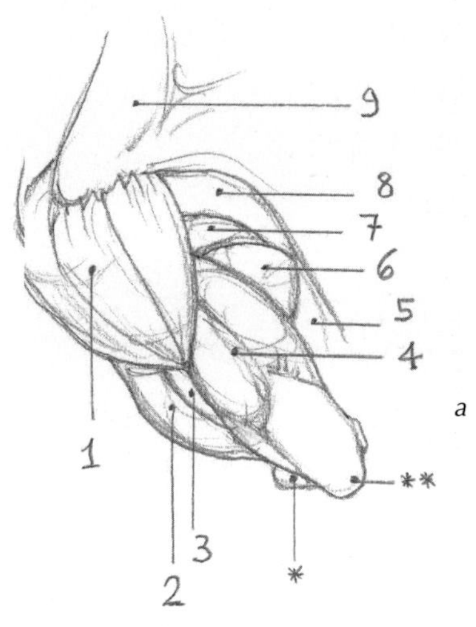

a) Shoulder

1 *Deltoid*
2 *Biceps*
3 *Brachialis*
4 *Triceps*
5 *Latissimus dorsi*
6 *Teres major*
7 *Teres minor*
8 *Infraspinatus*
9 *Trapezius*
* *Ulna*
** *Humerus*

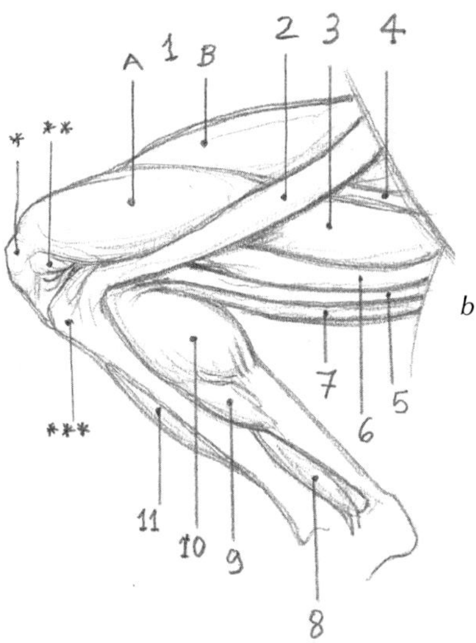

b) Thigh

1 *Femoral quadriceps:*
A *Vastus medialis*
B *Rectus femoris*
2 *Sartorius*
3 *Adductors*
4 *Pectineus*
5 *Semimembranosus*
6 *Gracilis*
7 *Semitendinosus*
8 *Common flexor*
9 *Soleus*
10 *Medial head*
11 *Tibialis anterior*
* *Patella*
** *Femur*
*** *Tibia*

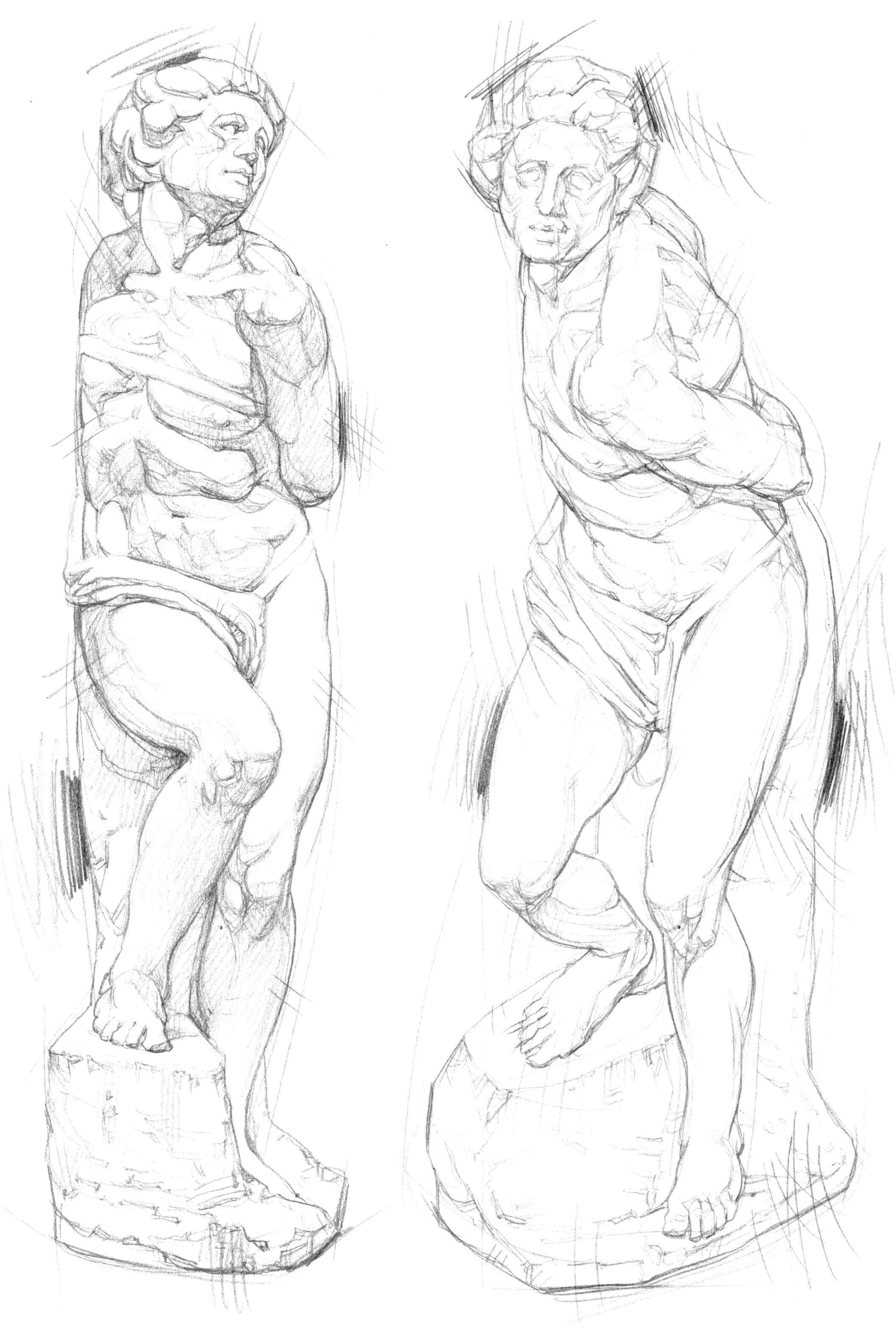

RONDANINI PIETÀ

Michelangelo Buonarroti (1475–1564), Pietà *(circa 1552–1564), marble, height 195cm (77in). Milan, Castello Sforzesco Museum.*

We know that this was Michelangelo's last sculpture, his final and perhaps biggest and most exciting work of art. The marble, thoroughly reworked over several years and in different periods, was the result of alterations and adaptations of a previous work, of which only a fragment in the isolated arm remains. The figure of Christ and that of the Mother holding him now seem to be a part of each other, thickened by the details, which are only hinted at. The movement seems to be upwards, from the base that originates in an earthly reality, witnessed by the concrete nature in which Christ's legs are sculpted; then ascending, gradually purified by the flame, to the evanescent forms only barely hewn from the marble, and rising into the transcendent state.

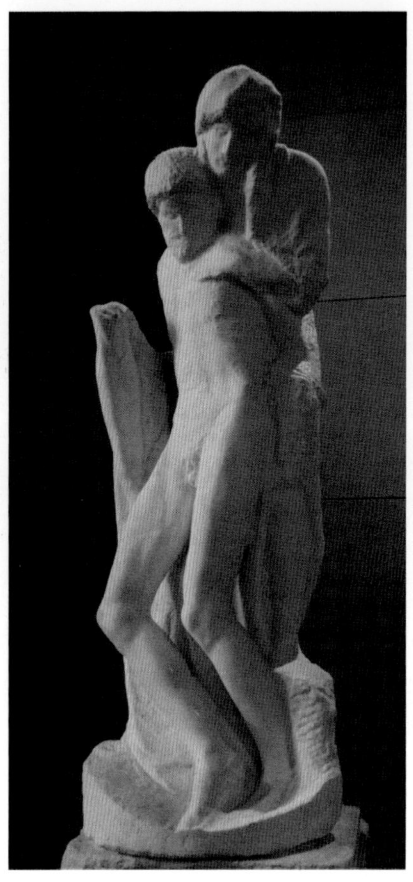

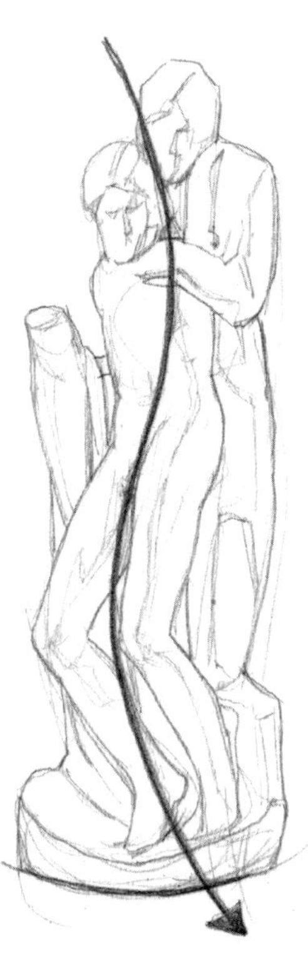

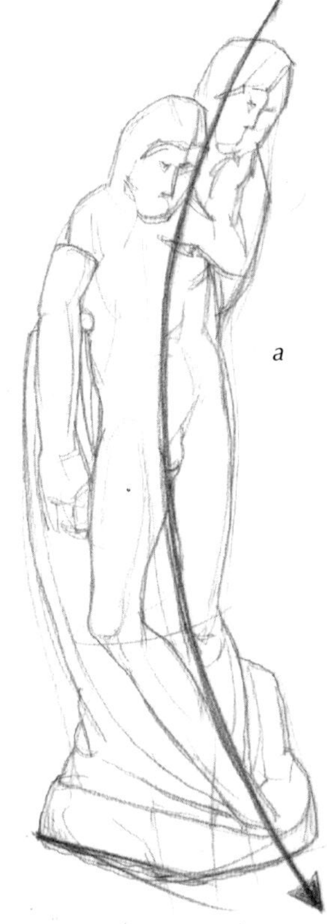

a

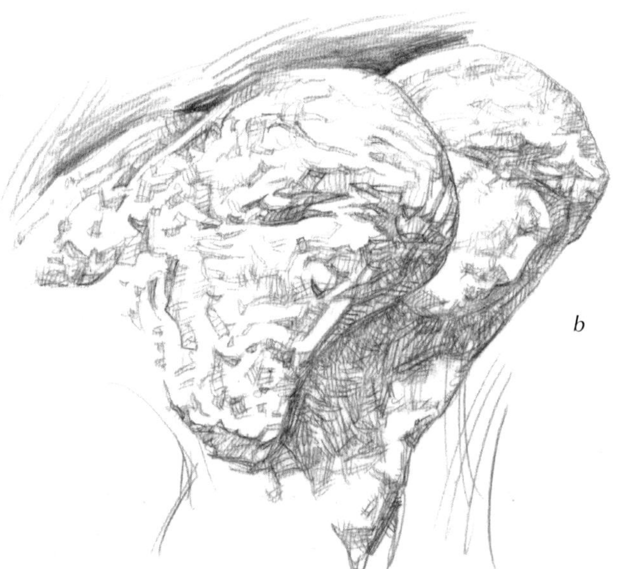

b

The composition of the sculpture (a) reveals Michelangelo's thoughts regarding movement, intended as a light, constant motion like the spiral of a flame. By looking at the different perspectives of the Pietà, *you can see some lines of an overall trend in the forms rather than an internal structure, which may seem to be distributed along curved or arched axes. During the Renaissance, in fact, works of art were structured according to precise, rational patterns, although not strictly geometrical (twisted and broken as in other styles), but shaped to the movement of the figures they represented.*

The single sculpture of the Rondanini Pietà *(b) contains and sums up all the techniques and procedures for sculpting stone, from the initial phases to the later more refined ones. The grooves and tracks left by the tools (tips, gradine, etc.) are a clear indication of the direction of the strikes, so that other less obvious forms can be seen emerging. Drawing can help to investigate the charming effects of structure and* chiaroscuro *(light and shade).*

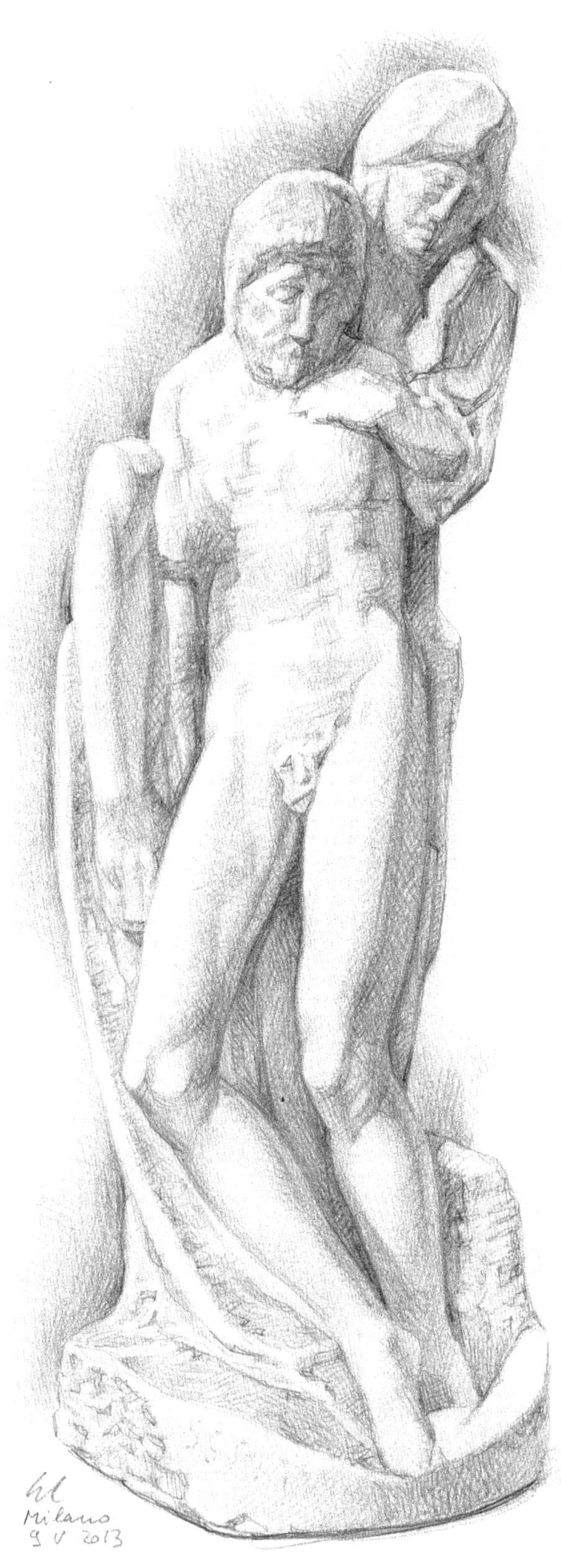
Milano
9 V 2013

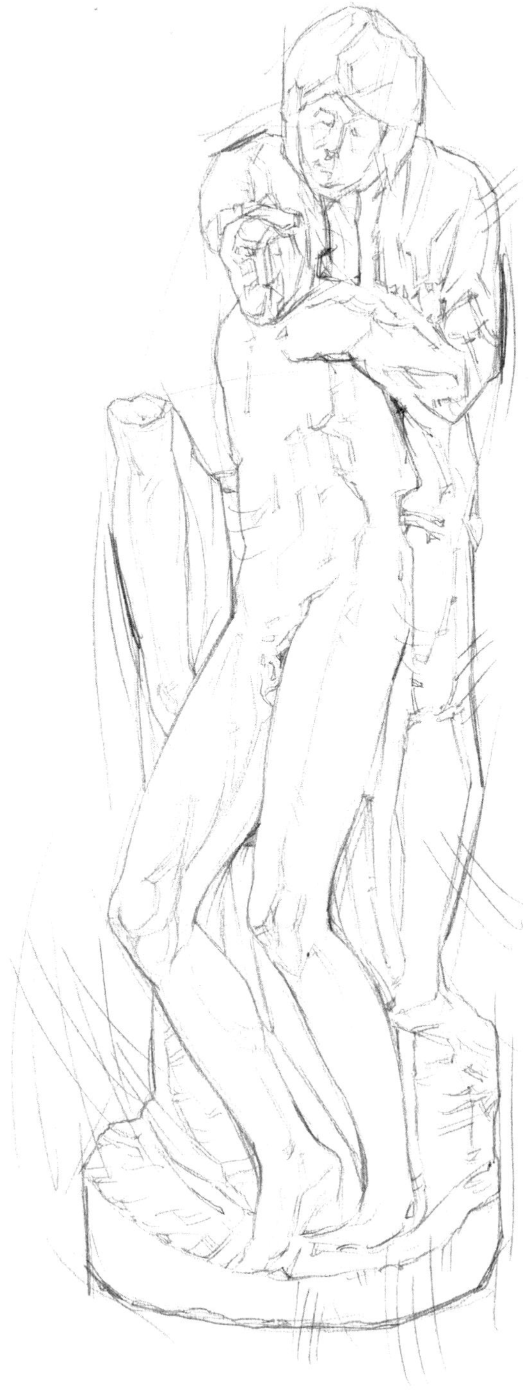

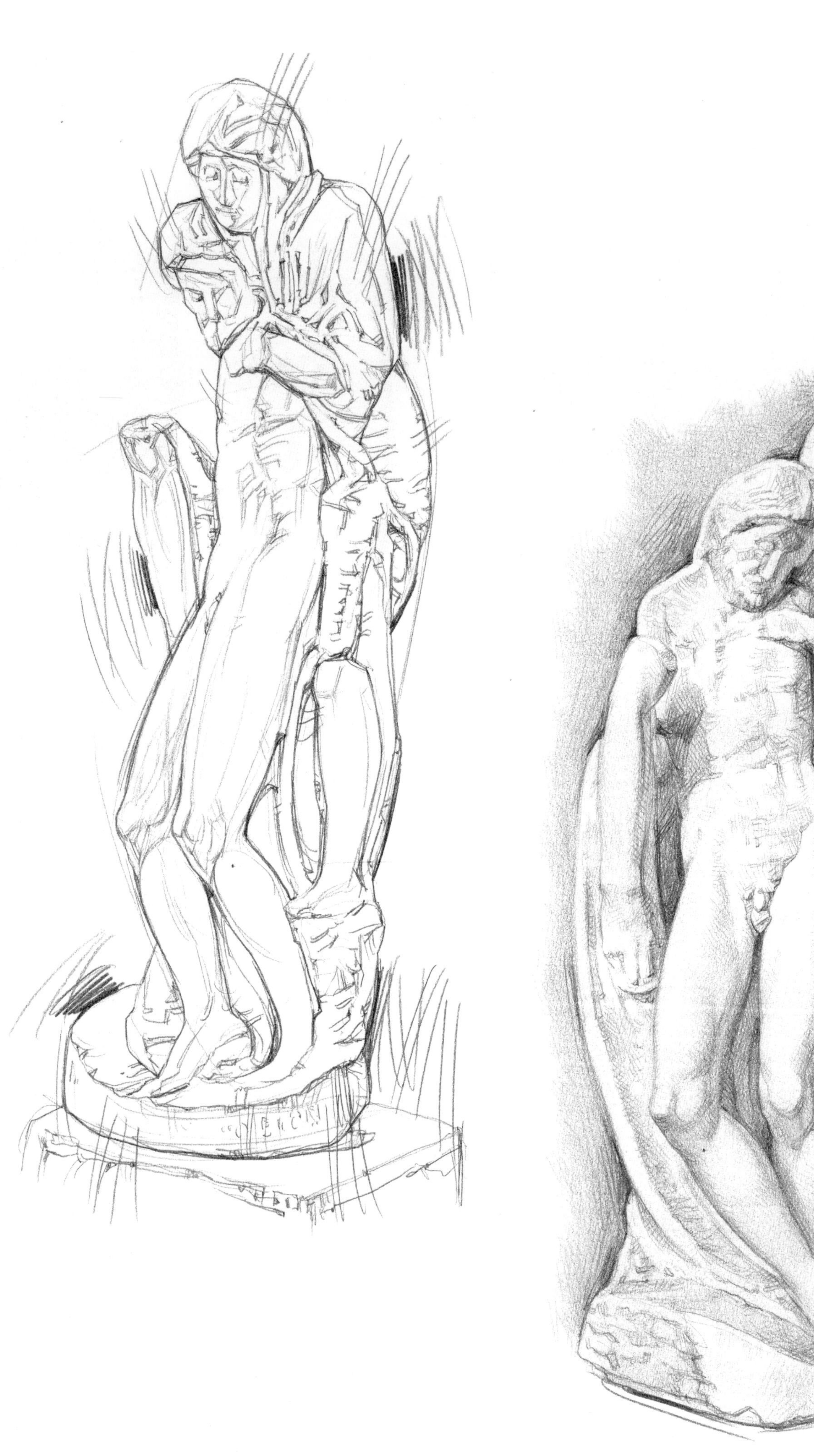

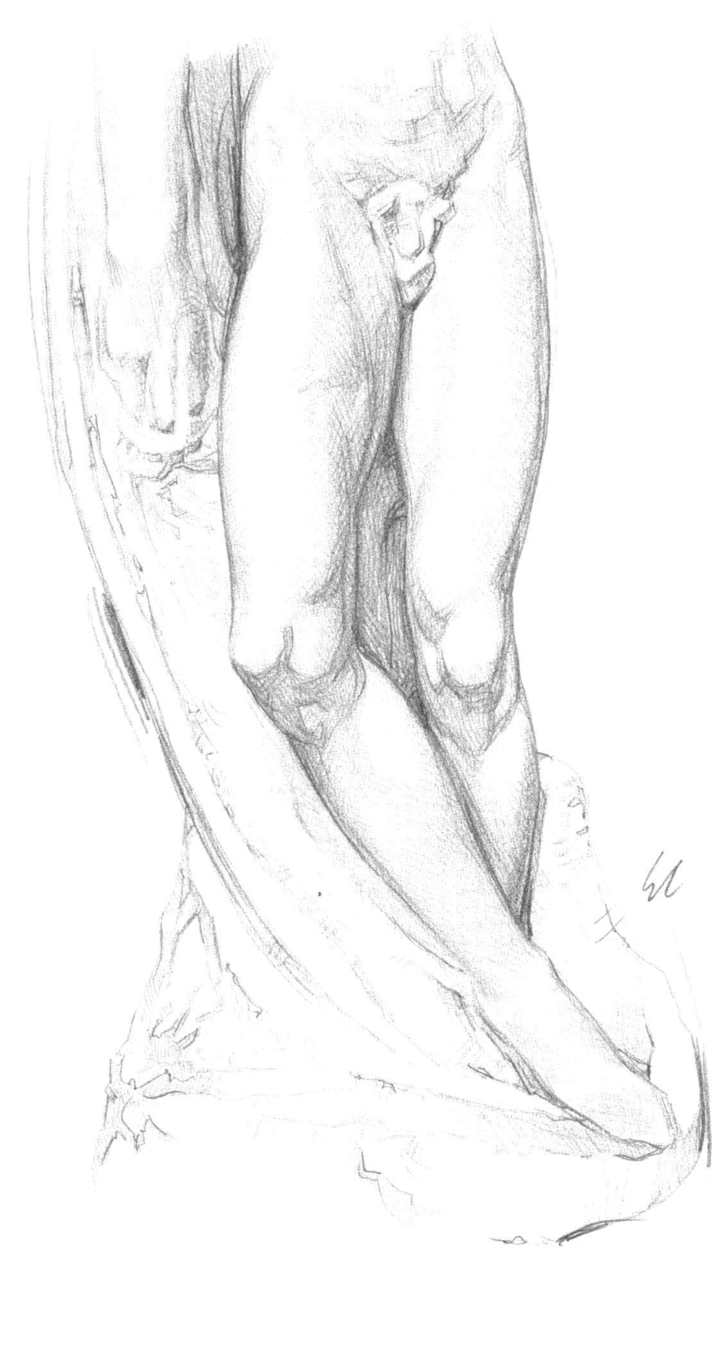

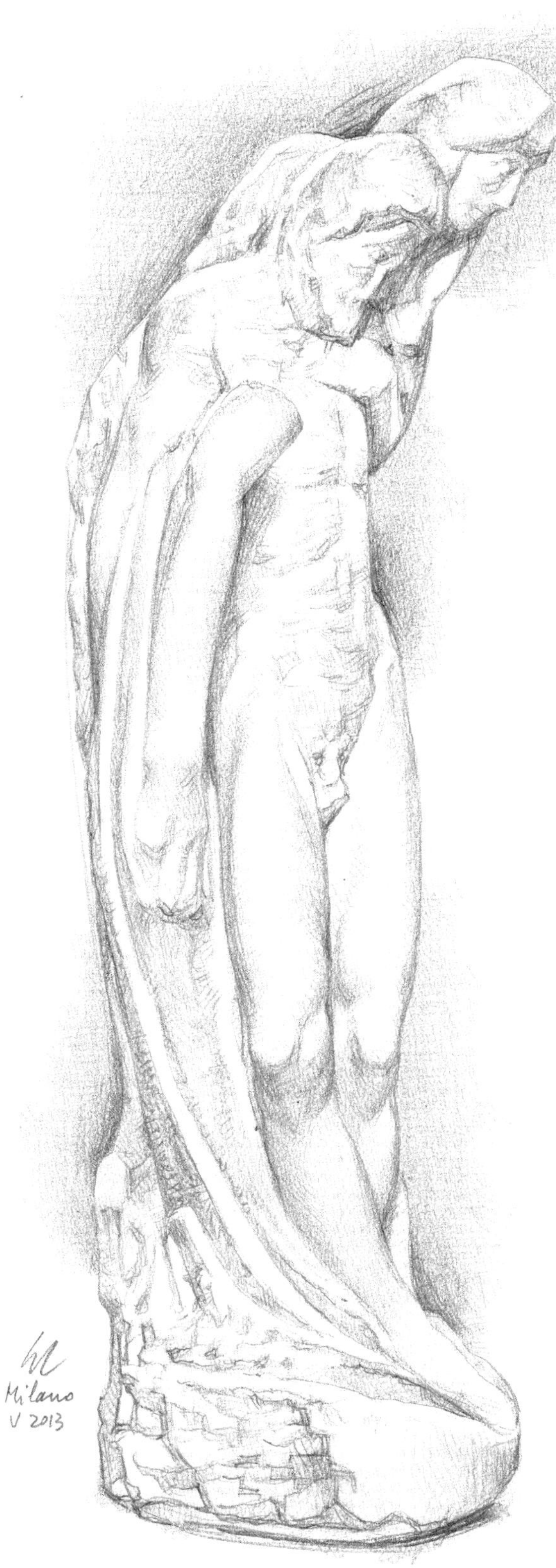

The delicate modelling style and detailed finish on Christ's knee contrast with the vigour of the chisel strikes that only dared to graze the remaining parts, leaving them eroded. Perhaps the deep hesitation comes from lending an explicit form to the inexpressible, both human and religious.

LITTLE DANCER AGED FOURTEEN

Edgar Degas (1834–1917), Little Dancer Aged Fourteen *(circa 1880), bronze and fabric, height 99cm (39in). Paris, Musée d'Orsay.*

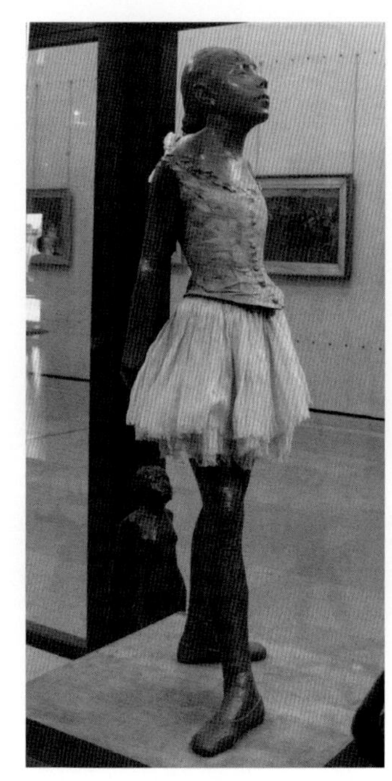

The original sculpture, kept in another art collection, is modelled in wax and also contains a large number of fabric elements, as well as a real wig, tights, corset and shoes. The statue on show at the Musée d'Orsay is fused in bronze and only the tutu skirt and the ribbon tying back the hair remain of the fabric elements. It is a small statue that is very interesting to draw, even if it is currently kept in a glass case that gives off multiple, overlapping reflections, making it difficult to effectively grasp all the light and shade details. The brown patina on the bronze also hides the modelling and the resulting tonal effects, which are expressed in the careful outlining of the profiles.

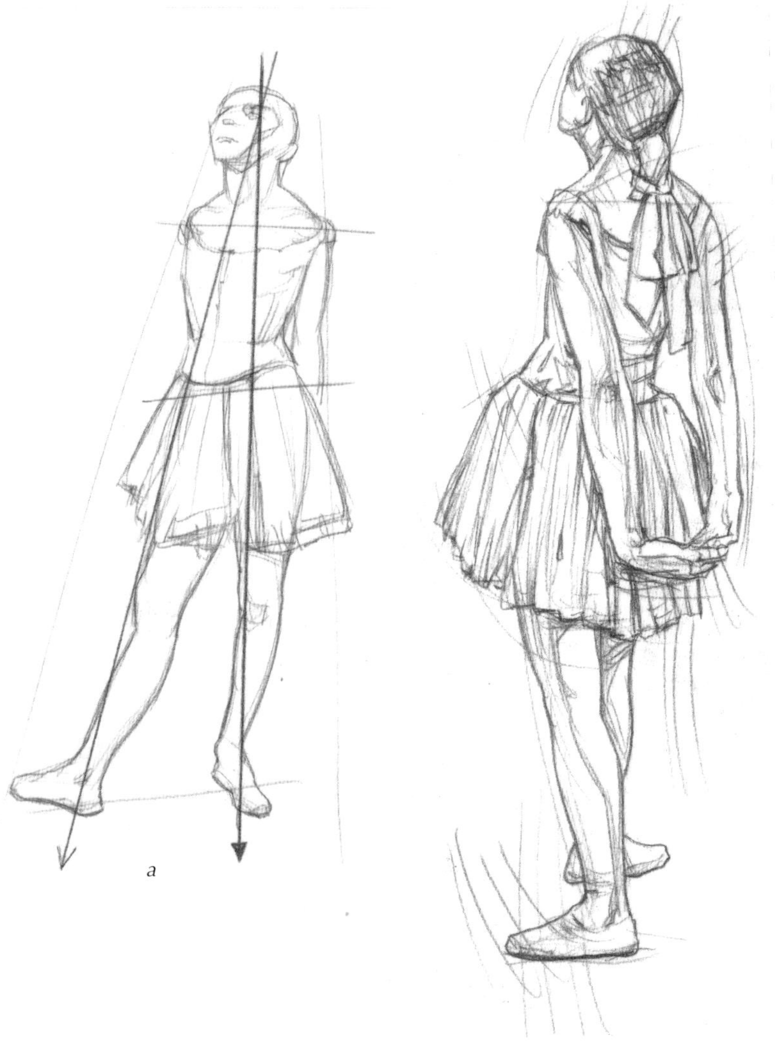

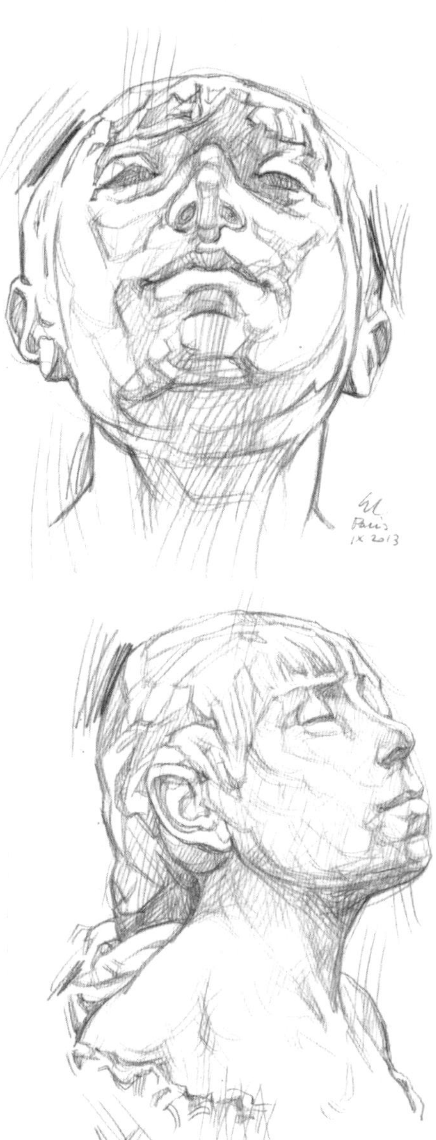

The position held by the dancer (a) is reminiscent of contrapposto *or counterpose in ancient art and it is emphasised by the dancer's separated legs and the right leg brought forward, with the pelvis consequently lower on that side. Her stance is inspired by the advanced natural position of waiting used in ballet and, although perfectly balanced, suggests a controlled dynamic tension.*

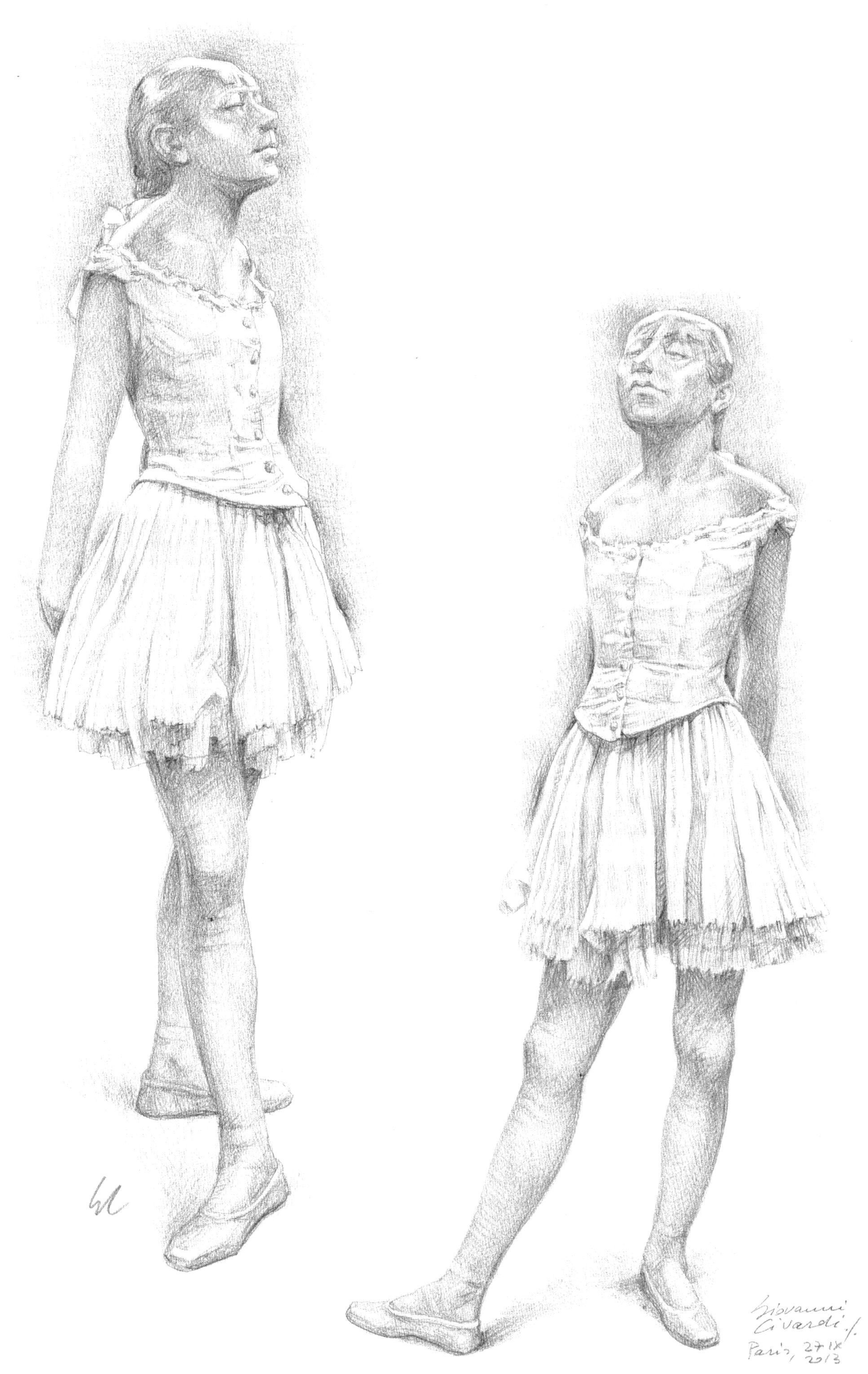
Giovanni Civardi f.
Paris, 27 IX 2013

THE KISS

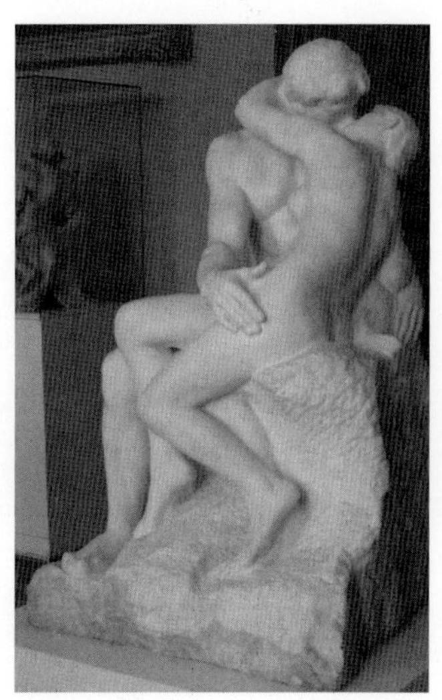

Auguste Rodin (1840–1917), The Kiss *(1889), marble, height 183.5cm (72½in), enlarged version of a terracotta sketch from 1881–82. Paris, Rodin Museum.*

The *Gates of Hell*, a momumental scuptural work, was a rich source of sculpture projects for Rodin, intended to test the existential condition of human solitude and the whirlwind passion of feelings, through intense and powerful shapes. *The Kiss*, however, was not included in the most advanced composition of the *Gates* (where it was substituted by a couple of bodies attached to each other in a more fluid, dynamic act), even though it was inspired by the love and death of Paolo and Francesca, so poetically described by Dante Alighieri in his *Inferno. The Kiss* was considered to be an autonomous group, enlarged at a later date to monumental proportions. The two lovers, surprised in their tender act which culminates in a fierce, desperate passion, are set in a position which means that, from whatever point of view they are seen, they have an expressive and decisive appearance. Drawing the forms of this sculpture is a stimulating, enriching experience, as it allows the artist to contemplate and depict the smooth, vibrant model of the bodies, in contrast with the roughly hewn rock base that they sit on and from which they emerge in an almost symbolic effort of moving from the harshness of raw carnal passion to the purifying sublimation of affectionate feeling.

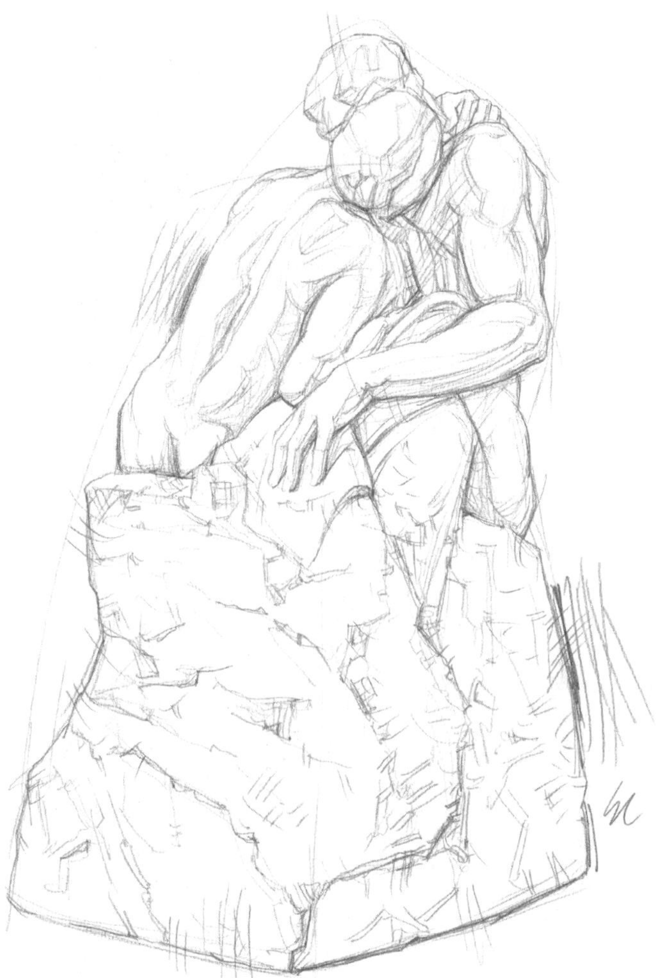

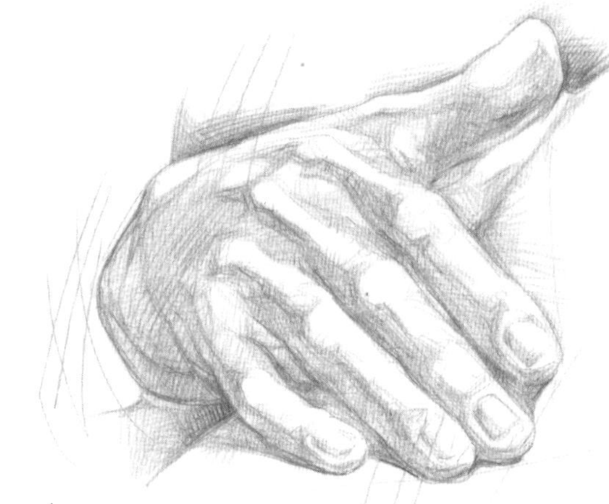

a

The fact that marble is more fragile forced the sculptor to use a few technical devices to provide support and strengthen the more delicate, thinner parts of the sculpture, such as the thumb on this hand (a). In addition to the complex form of a sculpture, it is wise to concentrate attention (and pleasure) on the expressive details. This hand is an example of that.

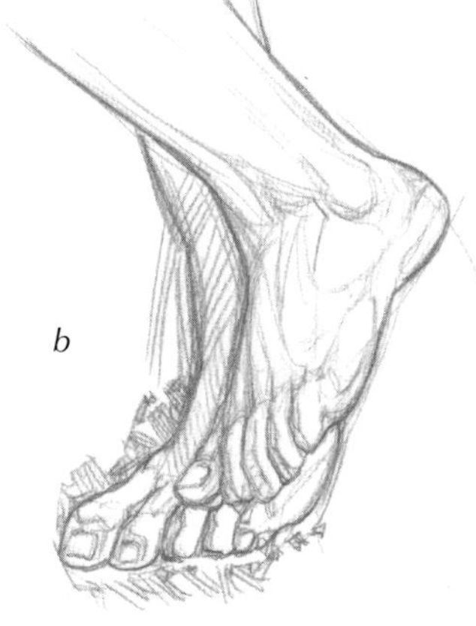

b

These drawings compare the male and female foot (b). This is an opportunity for considering the purely morphological differences and the proportions. It can also be a chance for the imagination to flow freely and dream: the male foot seems to be partly immersed in the rudimentary, muddy material, and over it, affectionately close, is the female foot, smaller and more delicate and relaxed.

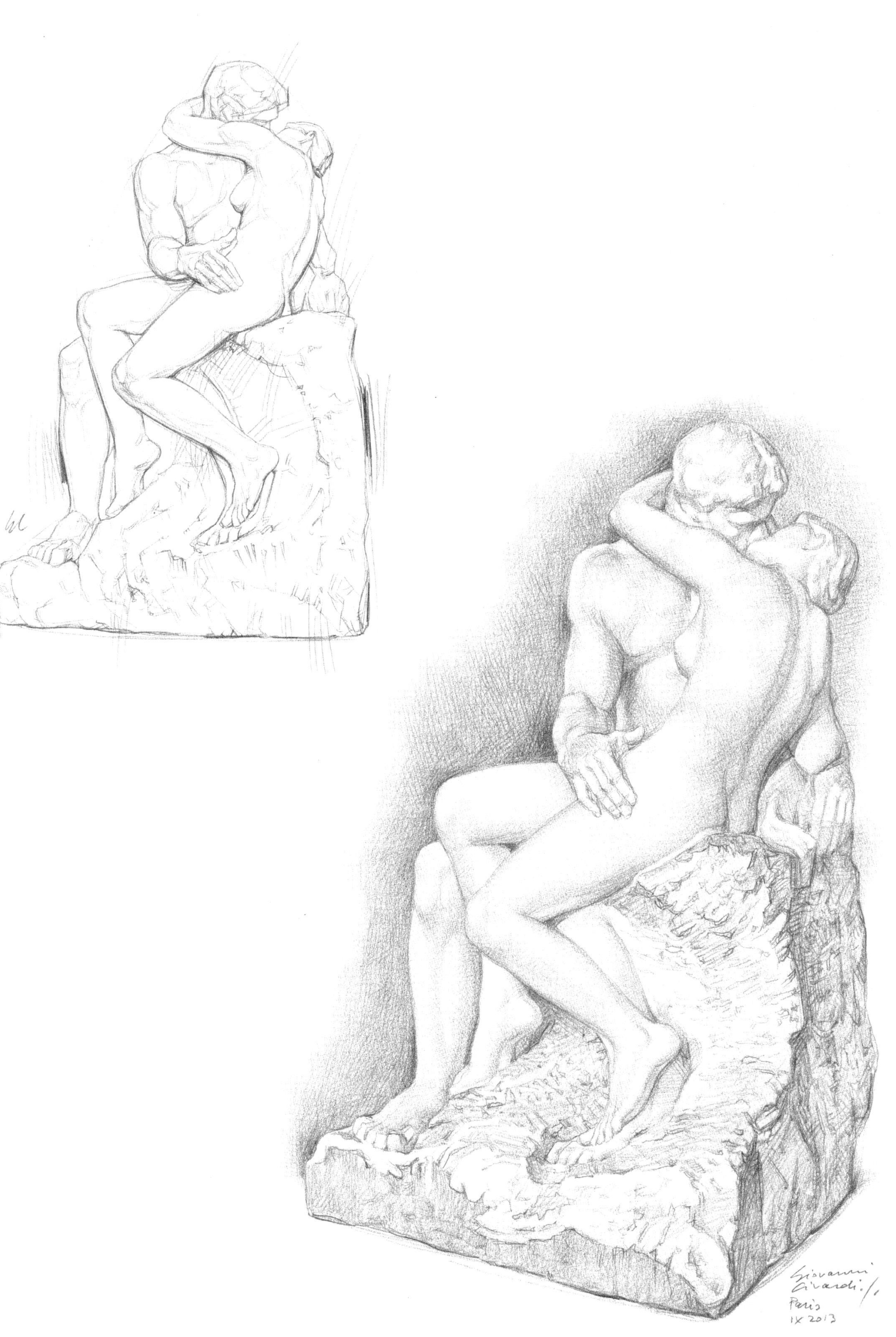
Giovanni Civardi
Paris
IX 2013

The way the bodies are wrapped around each other creates a spiral of tension that highlights the emotional affinity of their feelings and at the same time shows the difference in the bodies, i.e. the male muscular vigour and the clear fluidity of the female form.

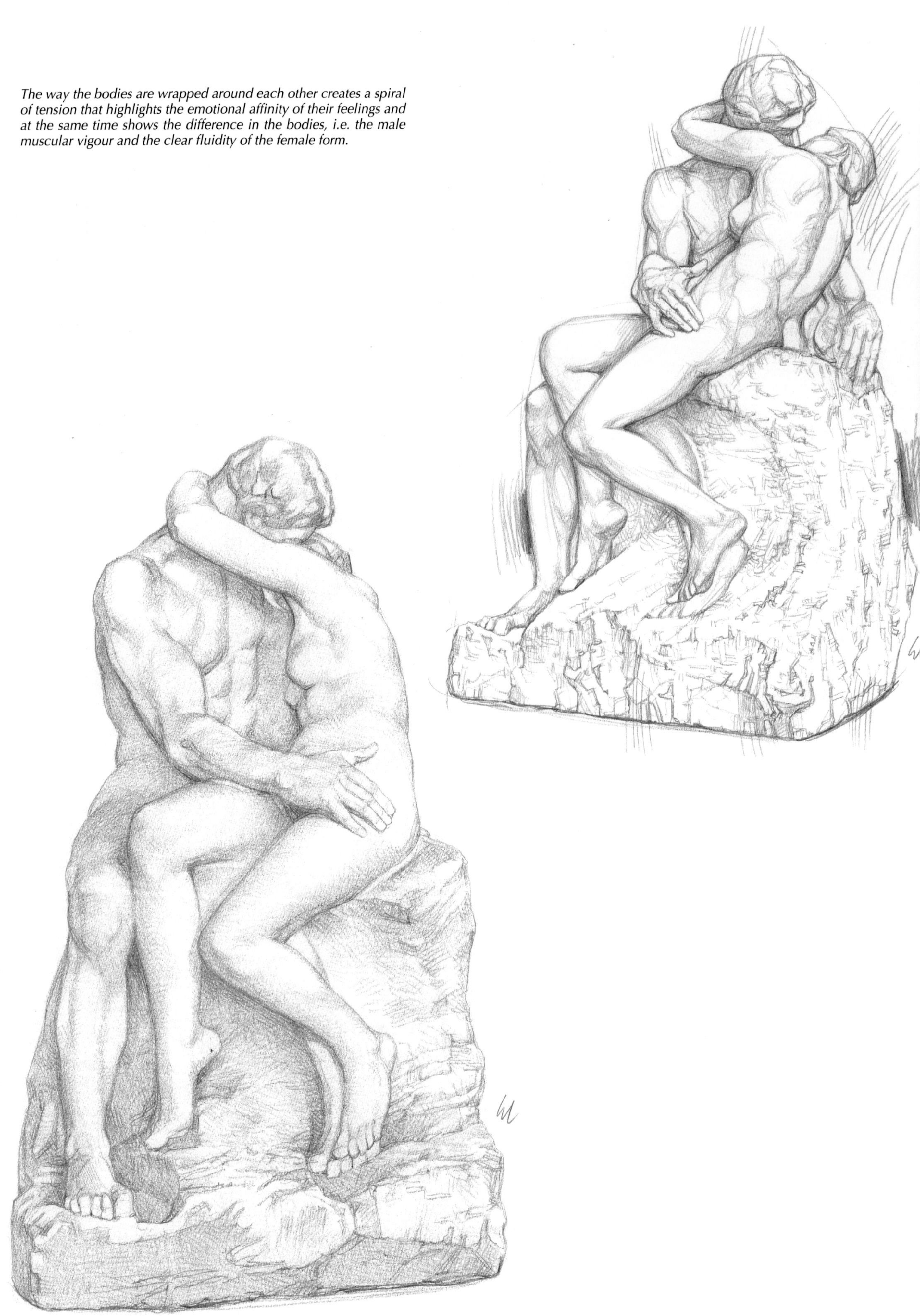

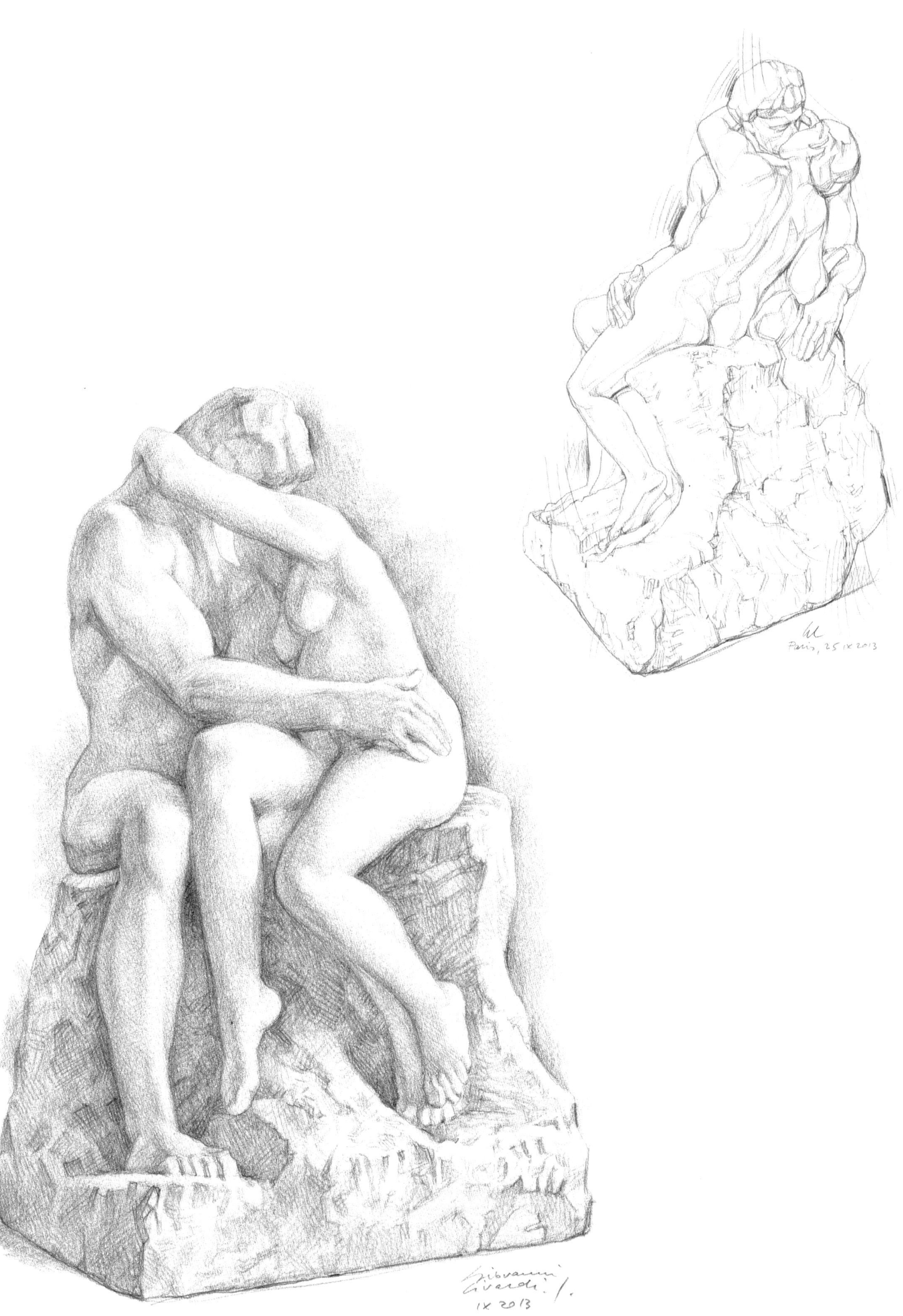
Paris, 25 IX 2013
Giovanni Civardi
IX 2013

HEAD OF HOMER

Imaginary portrait of Homer, Roman copy in marble of a Greek work of art from the 2nd century BC, height 55cm (21¾in). Paris, Musée du Louvre.

The autonomous sculpture of the head, (or bust-portrait, inspired by herma) was popular in Roman art, but was a rare event in Ancient Greece, as Greeks preferred a depiction of the entire body. This *Head of Homer* is an example of a reconstructed portrait, i.e. a representation of historical, mythological, religious, political and famous personalities from the past, whose actual features were unknown. They were imagined and reconstructed by the artist, who chose plausible physical features to emphasise the subject's personality and his physical, moral and psychological aspects, with the intention of celebrating his character.

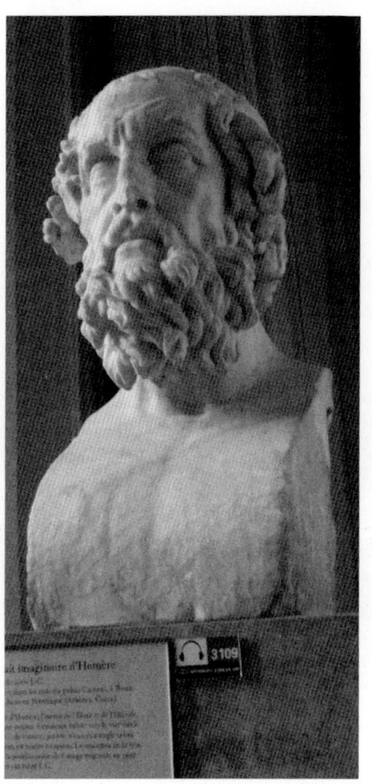

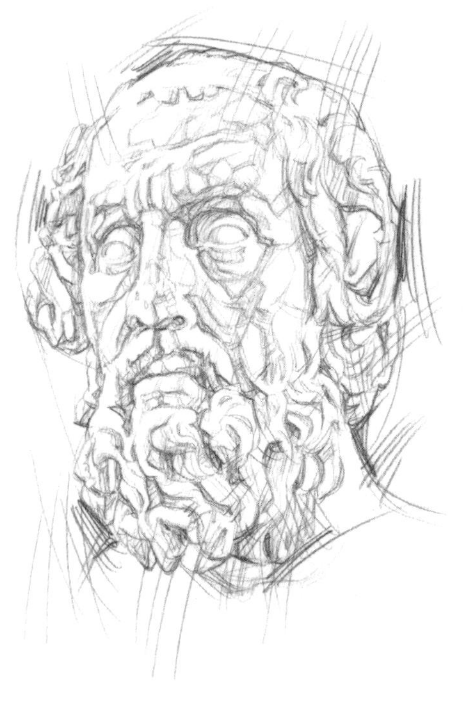

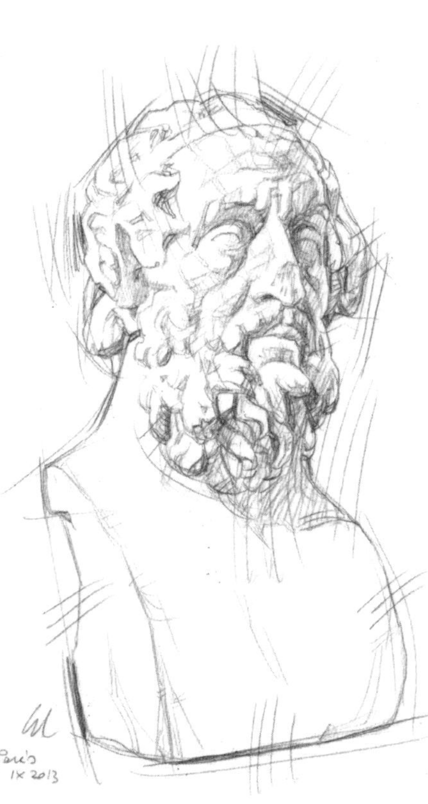

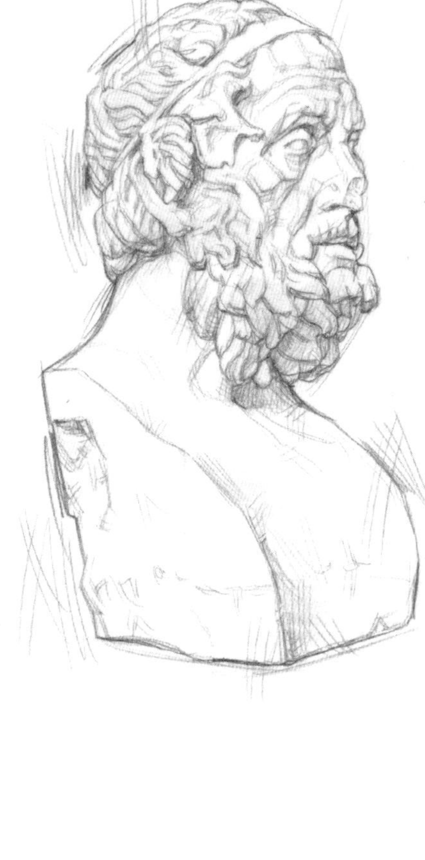

The sculpture of the Greek poet is wrapped in myth, and nothing much is known about its origins. Here, Homer is the blind epic poet who has always been described in scholarly tradition. The blind eyes are depicted with open eyelids that show an immobile yet vigilant gaze as though the poet is looking to grasp the tiniest vibrations of the mind. The wrinkles on his face are a symbol of deep thought. His short hair, tied with a band, is wavy like his thick beard, and both are moved by the wind of inspiration.

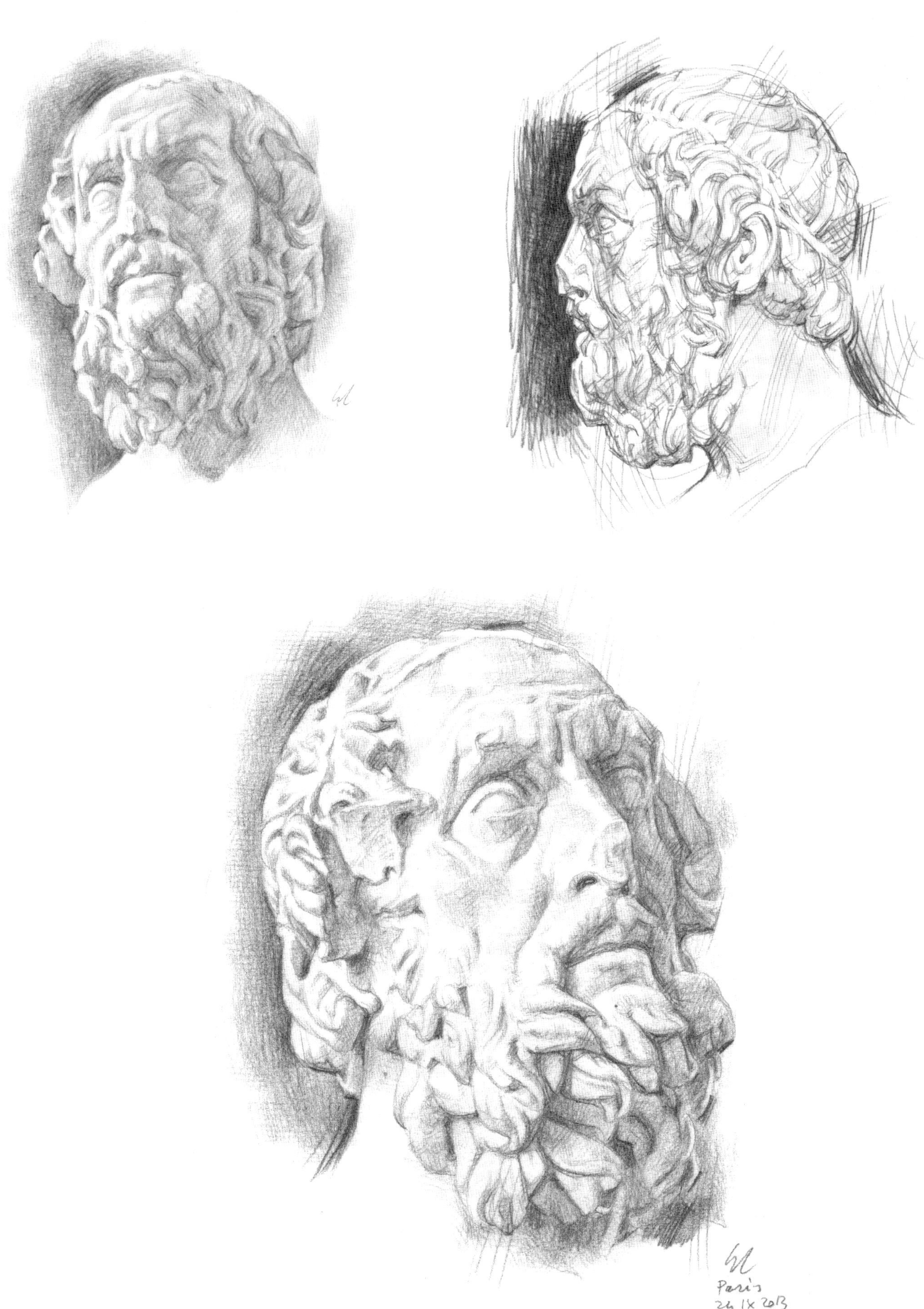
Paris
24 IX 2013

SKETCHBOOK STUDIES

On the previous pages of this book there are some drawings that I created specifically, using a slightly structural, didactic system, in order to highlight some of the interesting aspects for the formal analysis of each statue. After a bit of practice, it will be easy for anyone to achieve a stylistically more personal style which is aesthetically more artistic. I drew all these sketches in a notebook that is 21.5 x 27.5cm (8½ x 11in), using medium grade (HB and 2B) graphite pencils. In this section, on the other hand, I have chosen to show you some pages from my sketchbooks that are of a more liberal, inquisitive nature, carried out at different times, in varying circumstances and conditions, as more intimate notes on the emotions, study subjects and effects. These pages are a kind of visual diary that each artist, regardless of his or her style, should fill out almost every day, in the frankest way, to nurture and increase the expressive art he or she aspires to perfect. The photograph shows an artist doing just this at the Louvre.

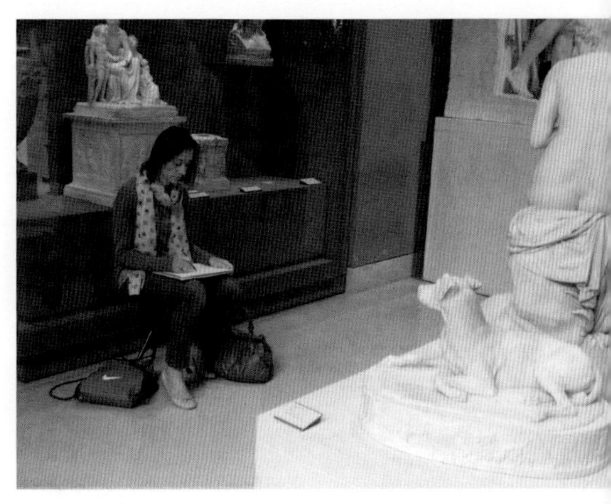

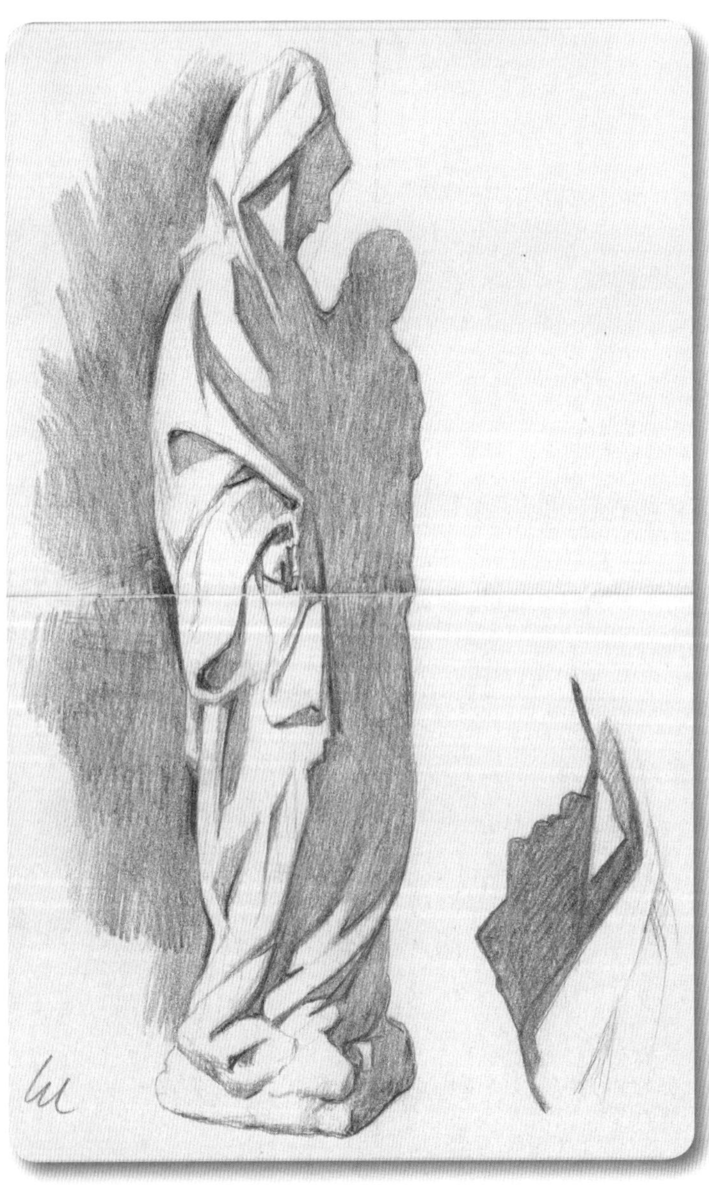

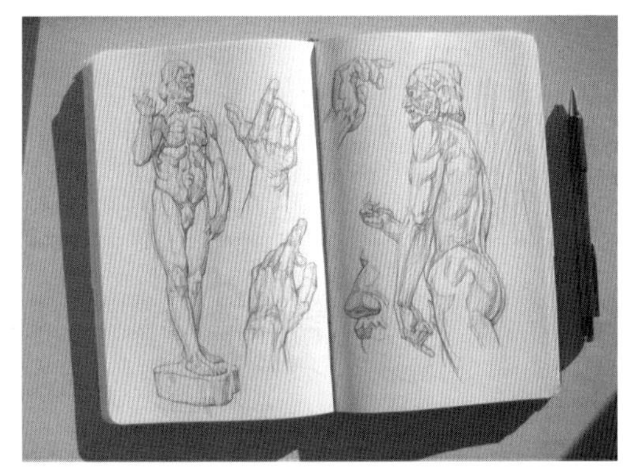

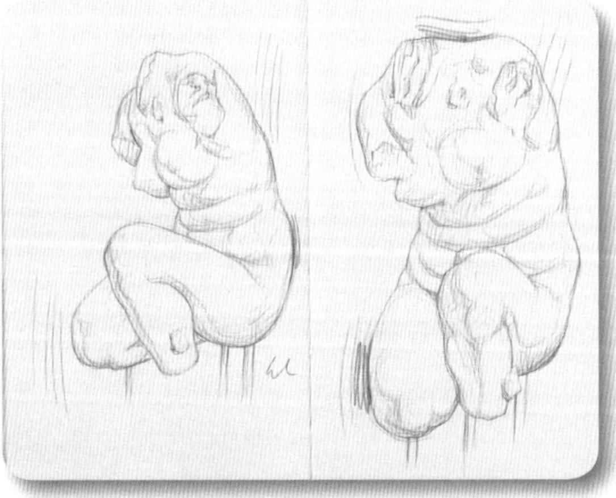

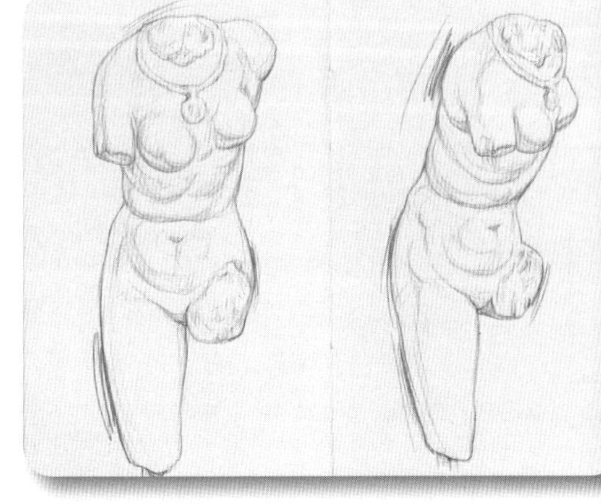

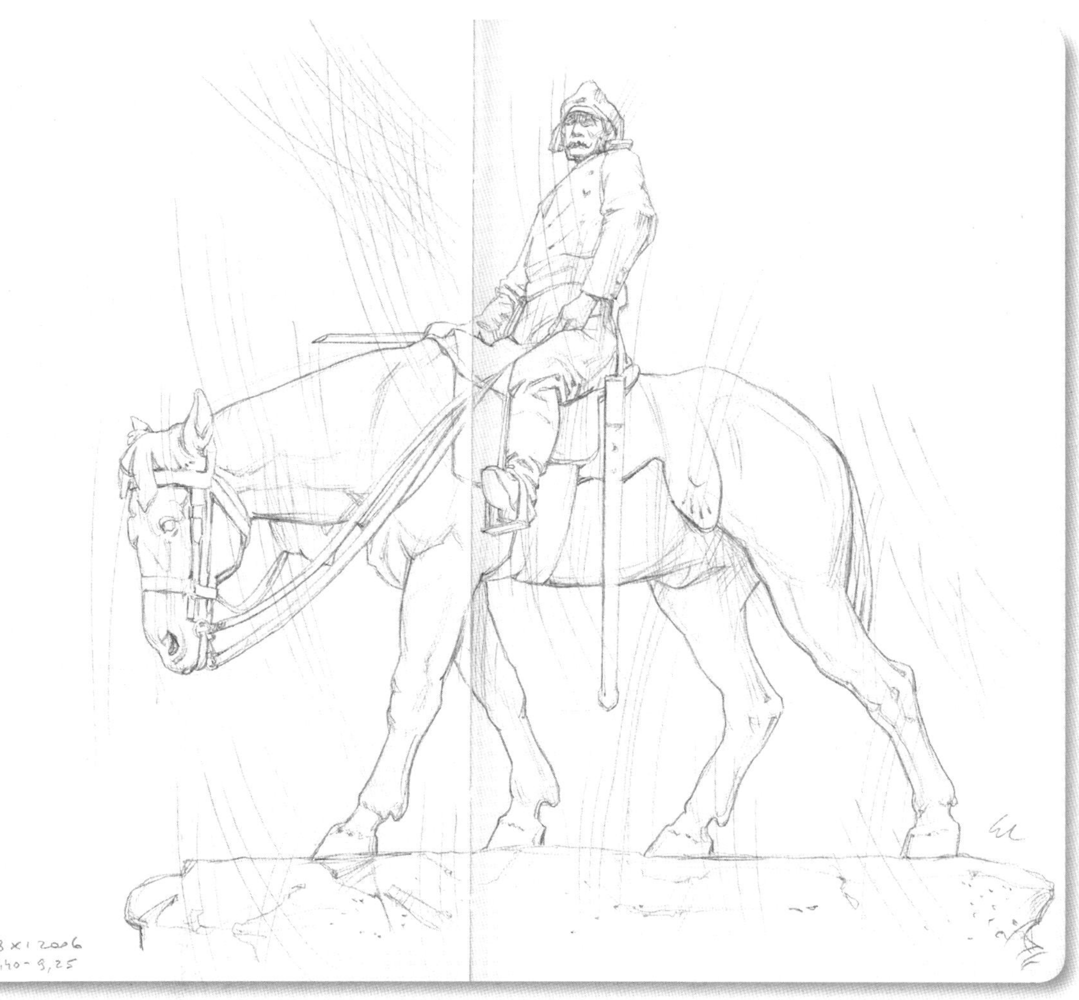

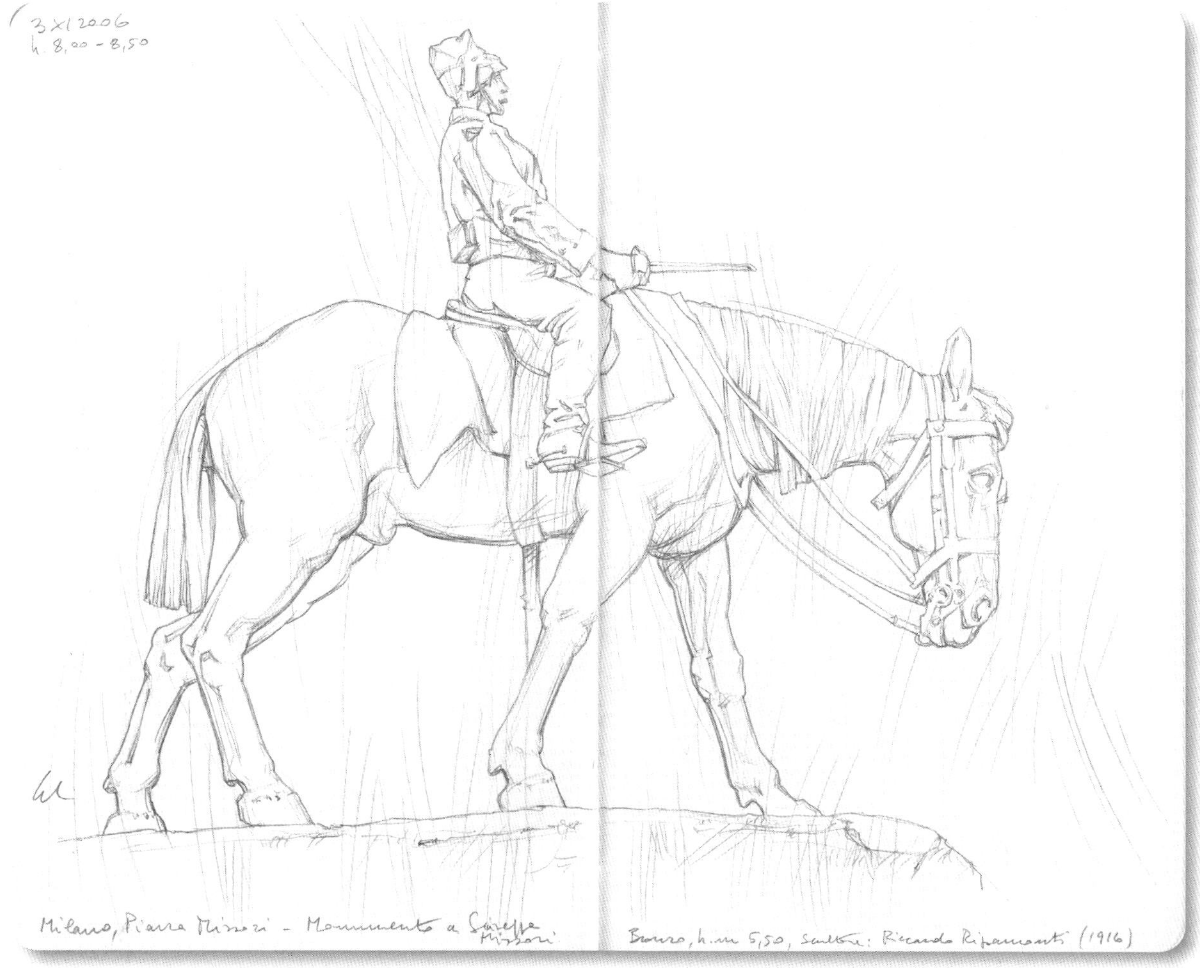

3 X I 2006
h. 8,00 - 8,50

Milano, Piazza Missori - Monumento a Giuseppe Missori

Bronzo, h. m 5,50, Scultore: Riccardo Ripamonti (1916)

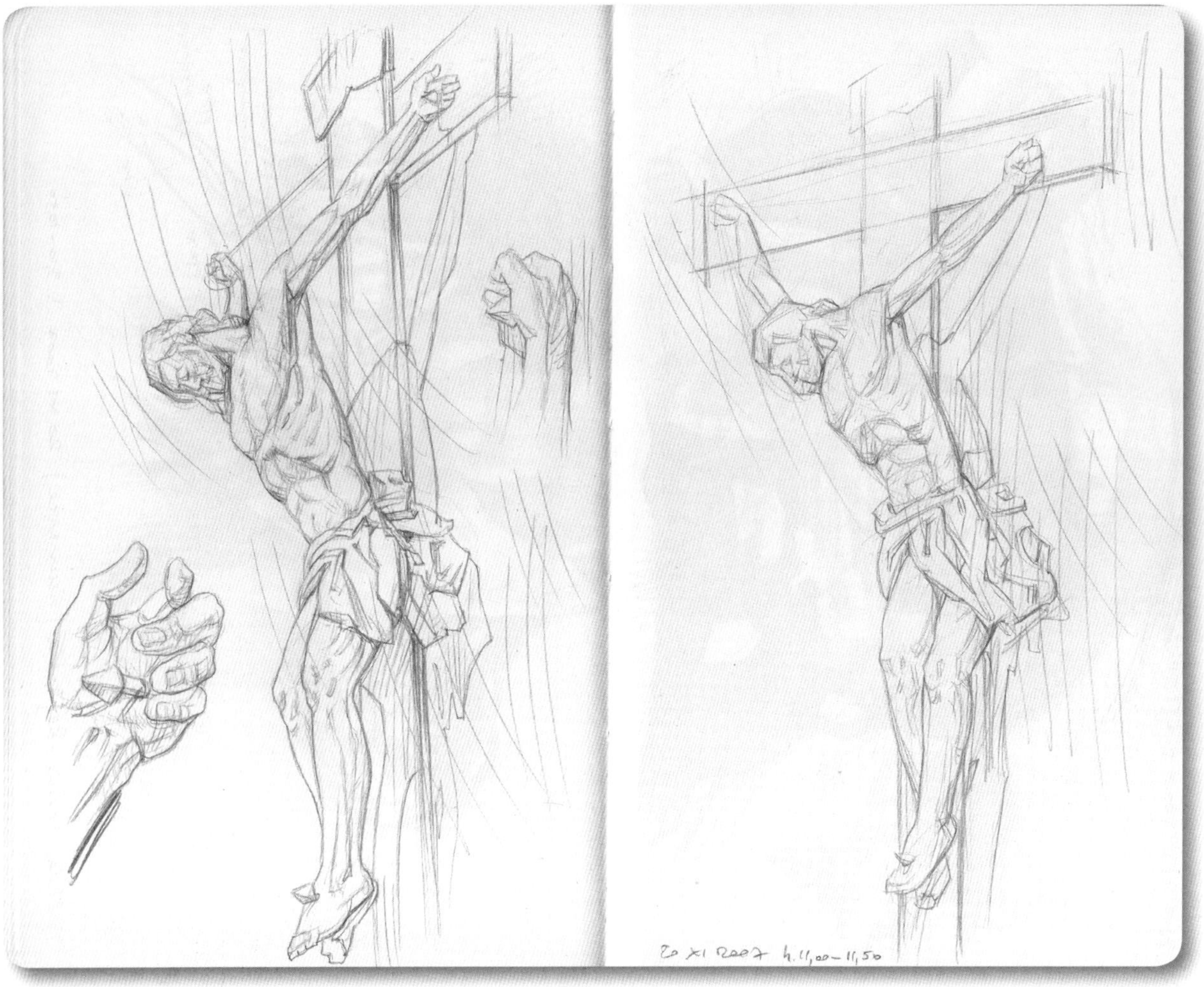

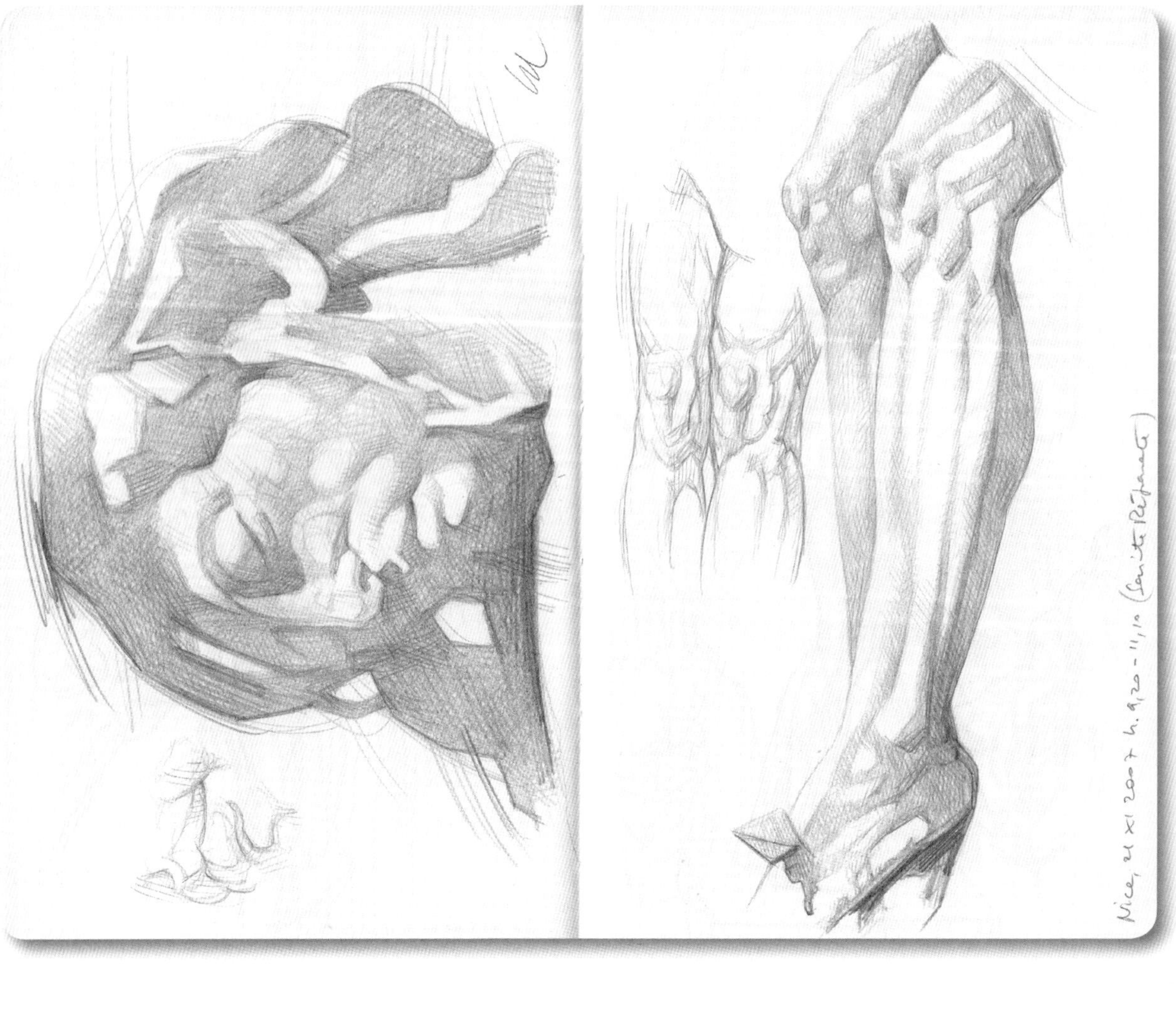

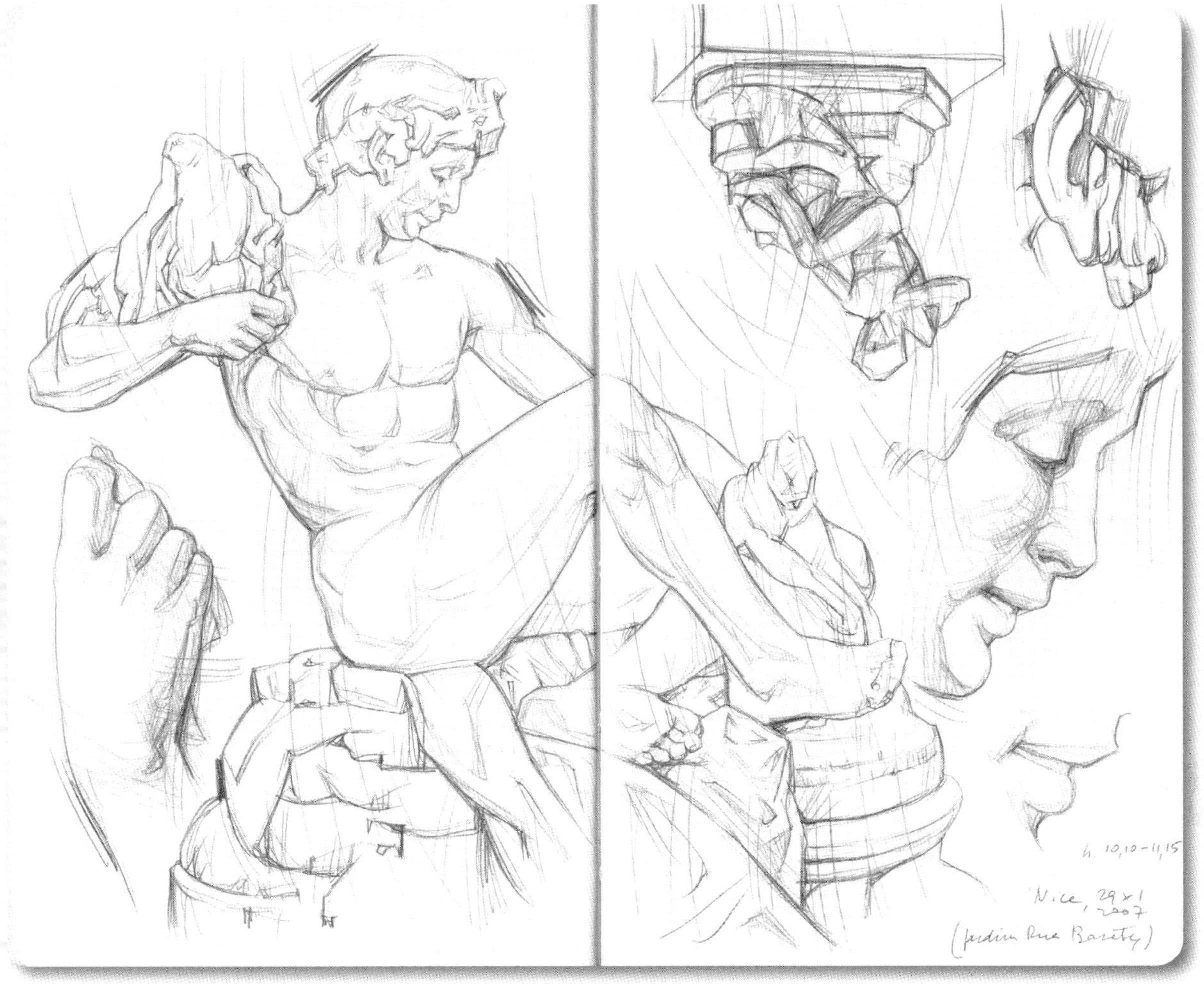

h. 10,10–11,15

Nice, 29 x I 2007

(Jardin Rue Barety)

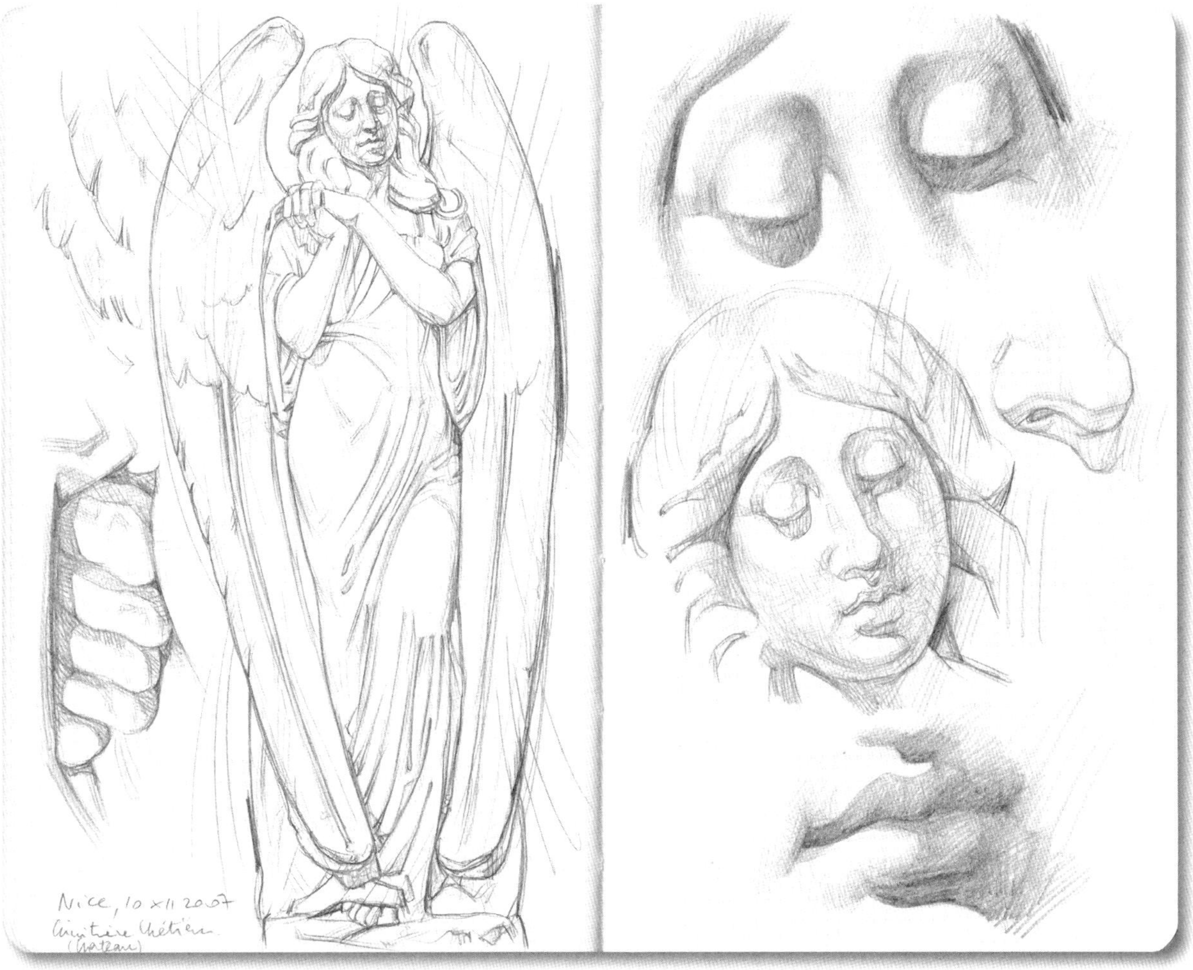

Nice, 10 x II 2007

Cimetière Chrétien

(Château)

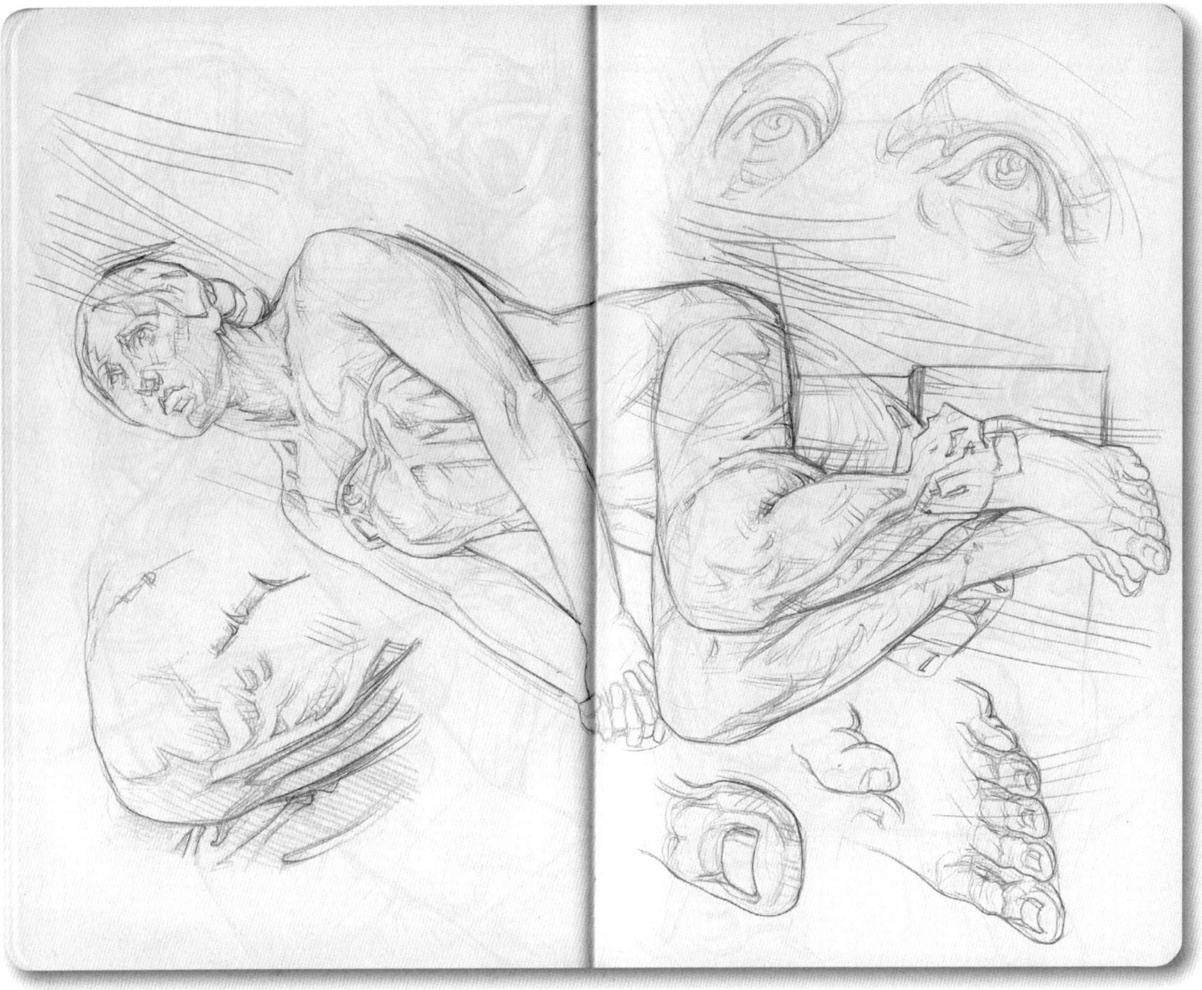

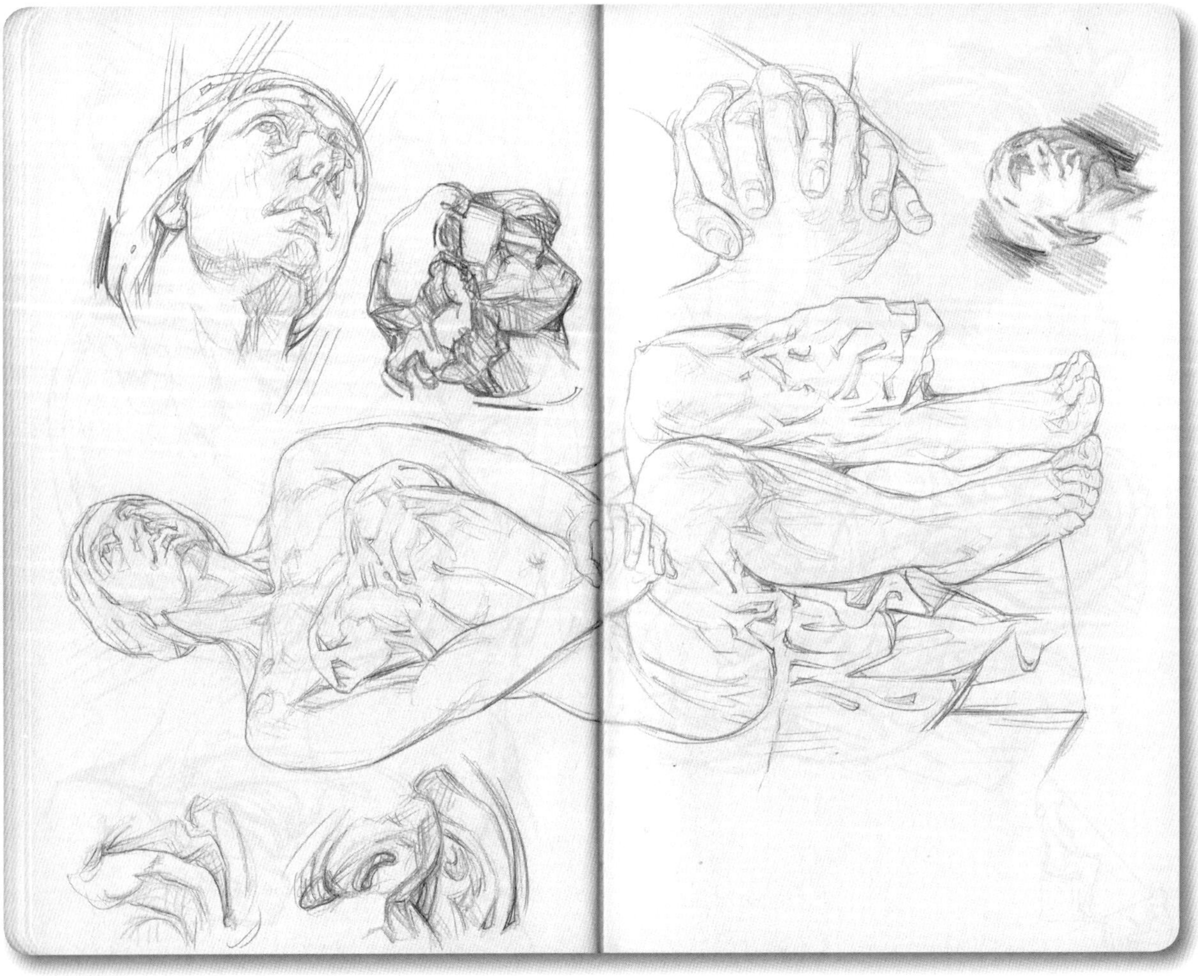

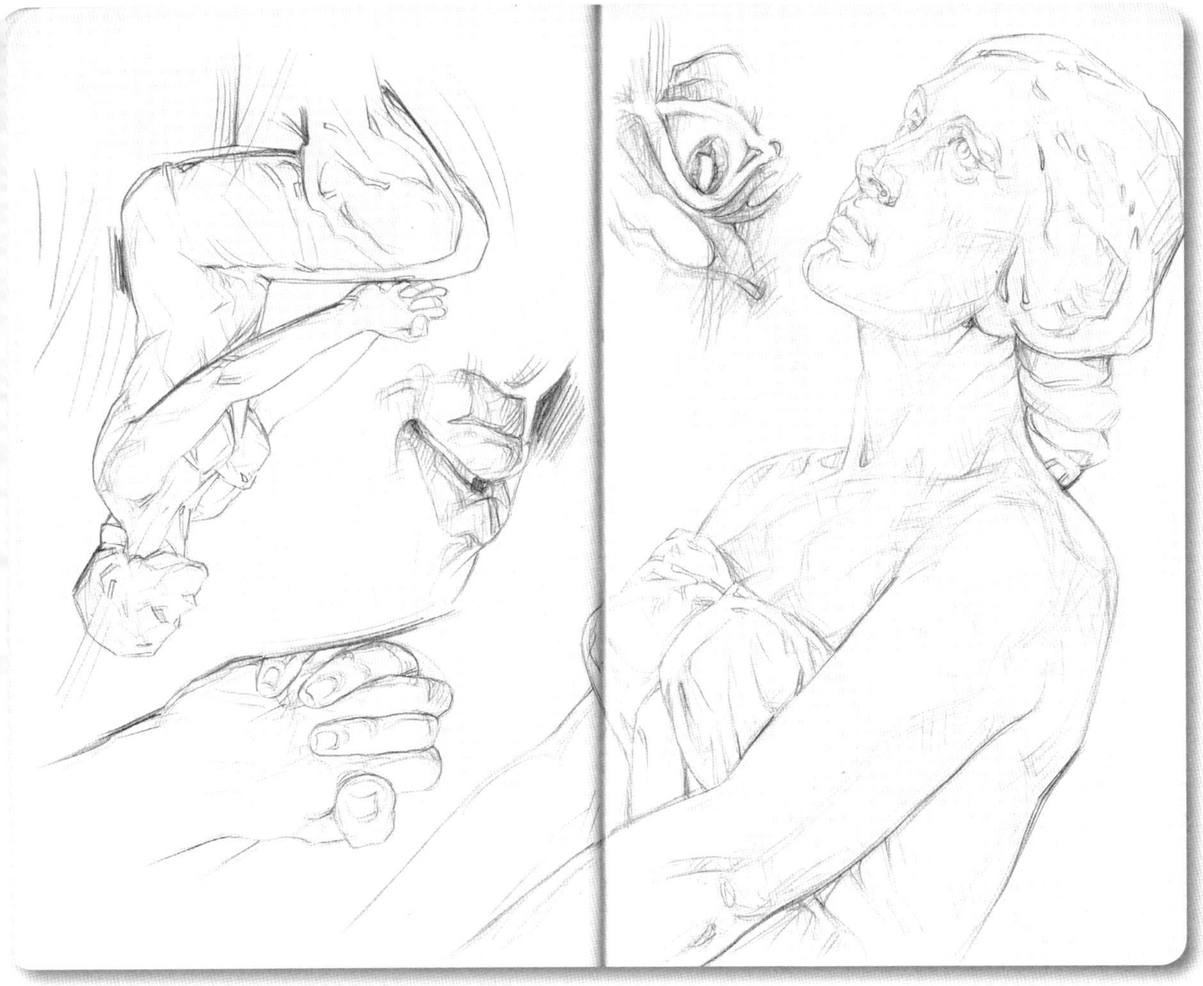

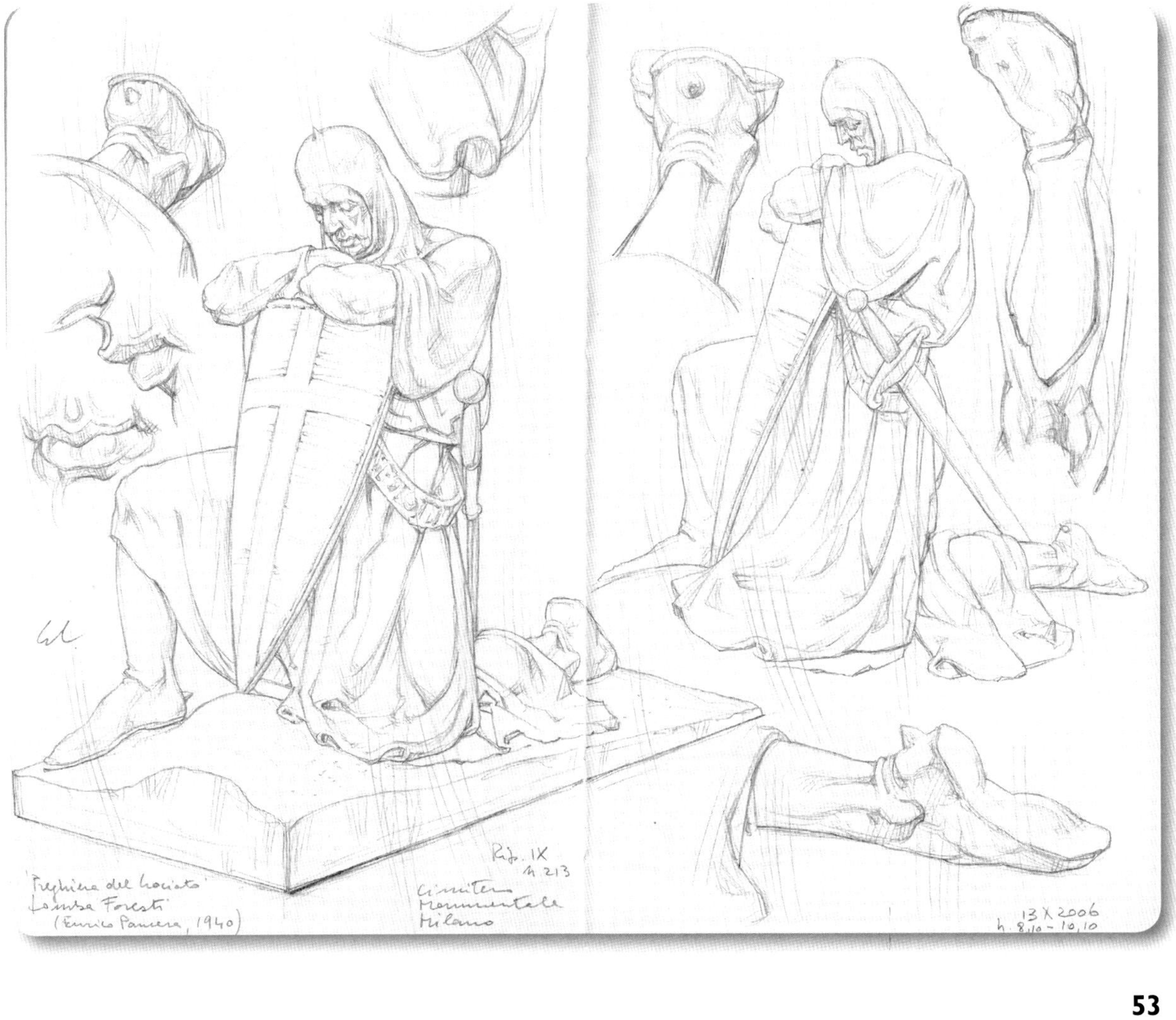

'Preghiera del Crociato'
Tomba Foresti
(Enrico Pancera, 1940)

Rip. IX
n. 213

Cimitero
Monumentale
Milano

13 X 2006
h. 8,10 – 10,10

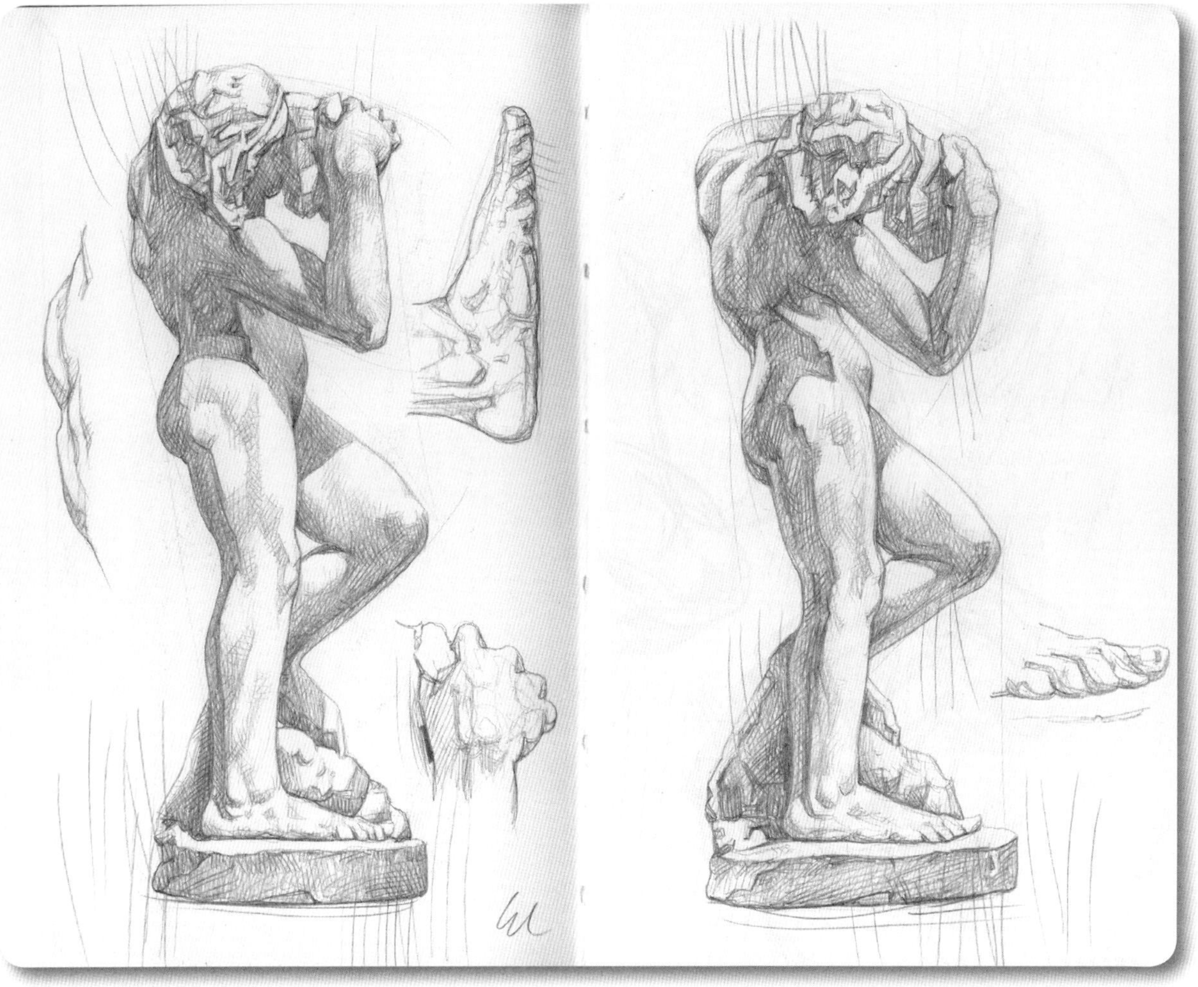

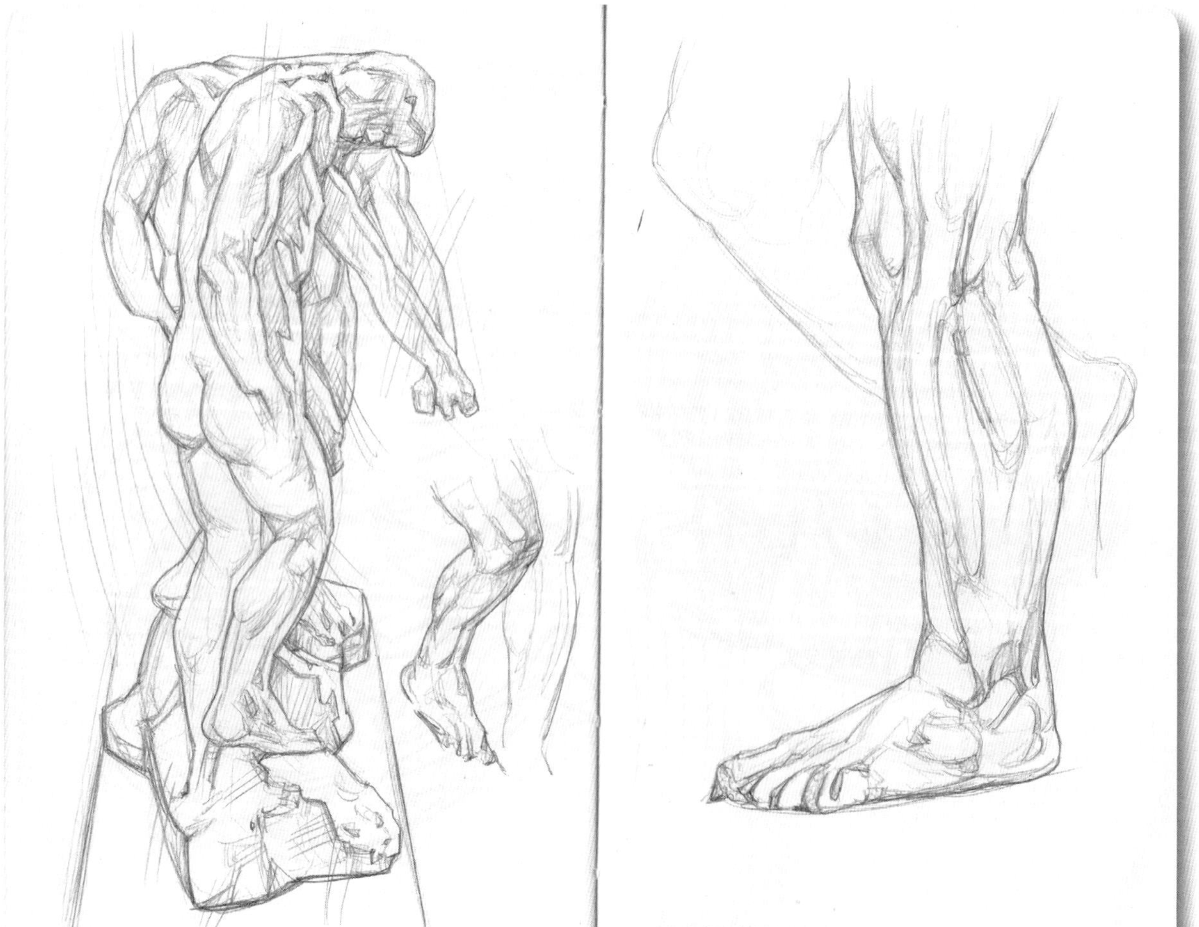

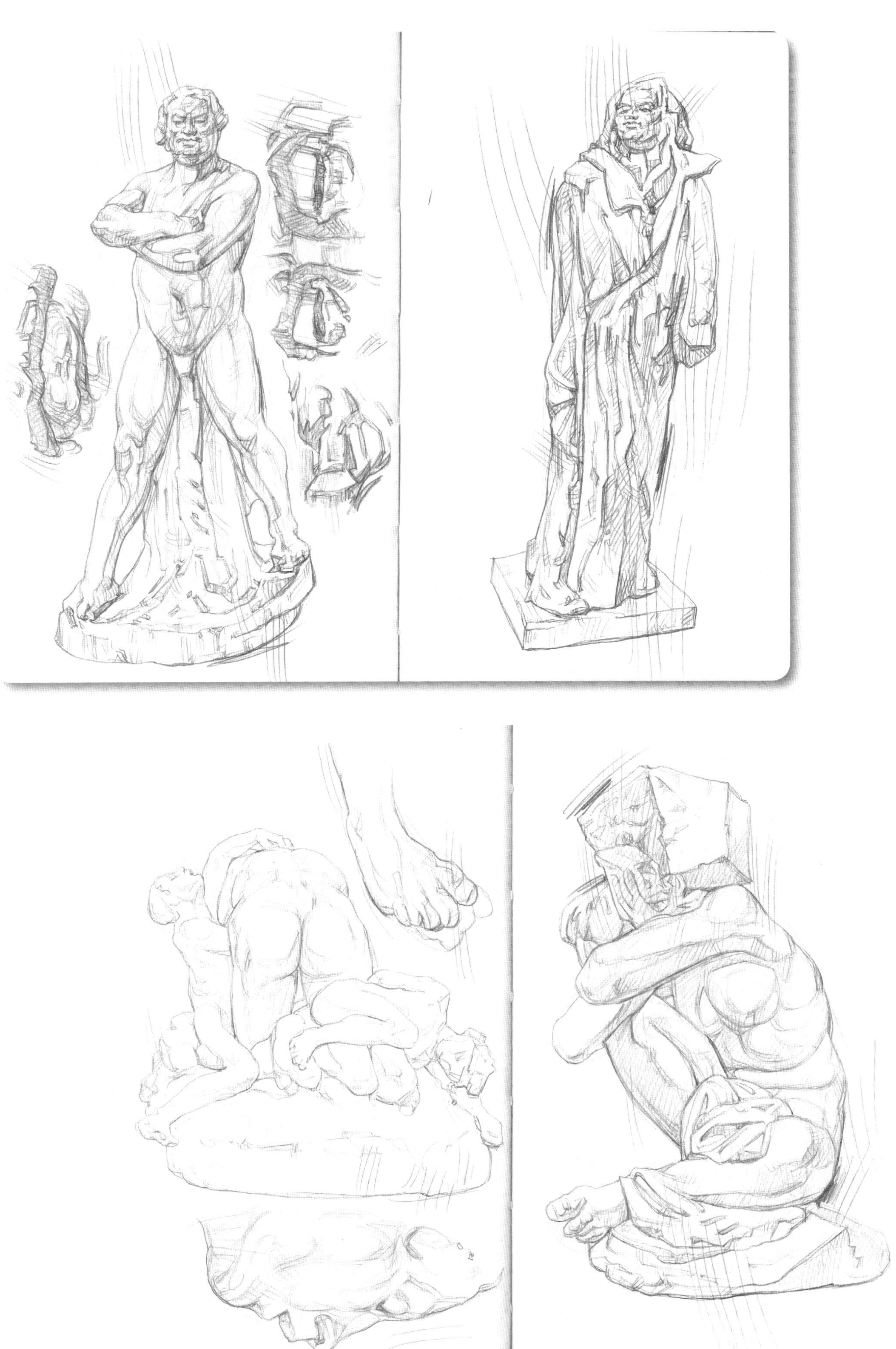

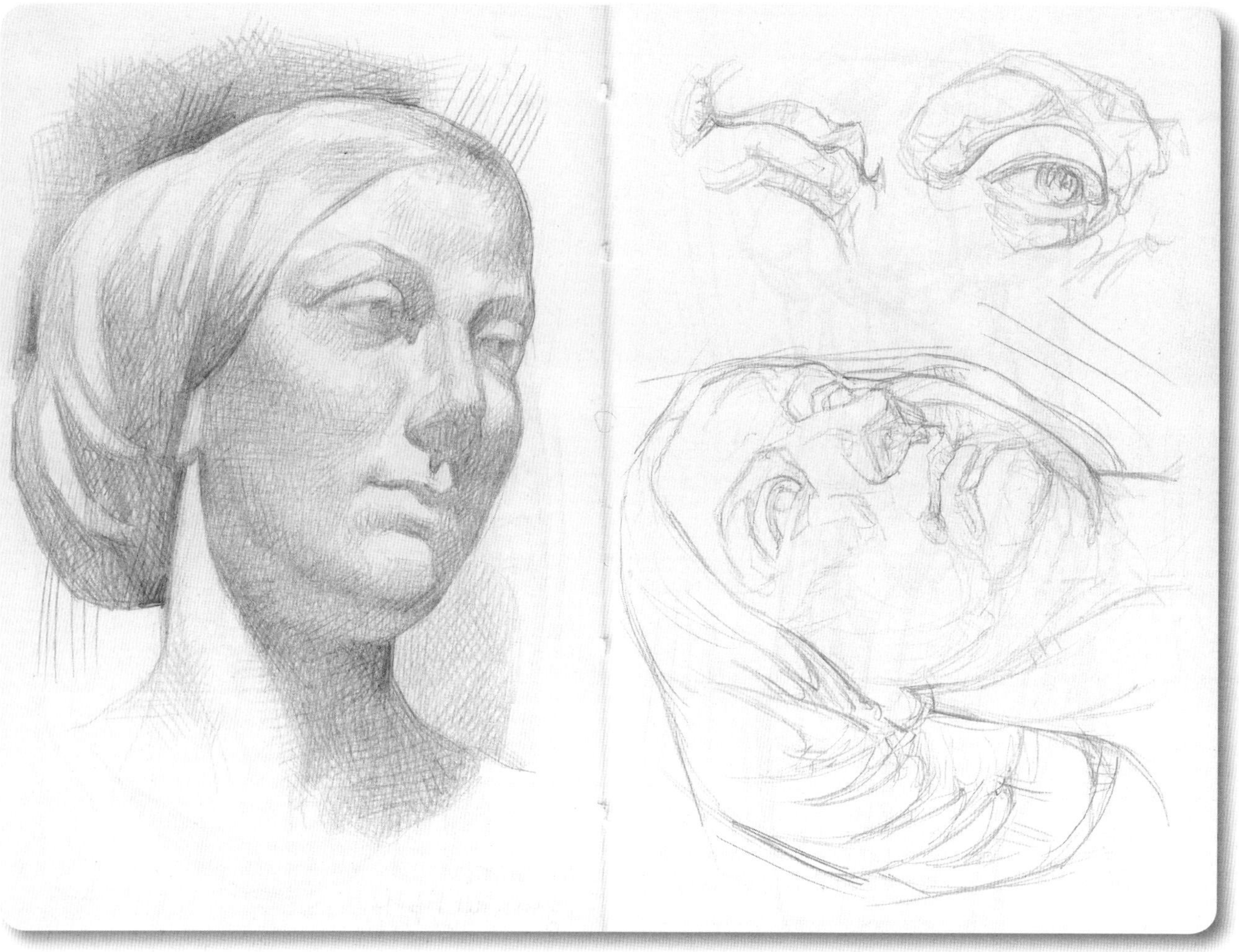

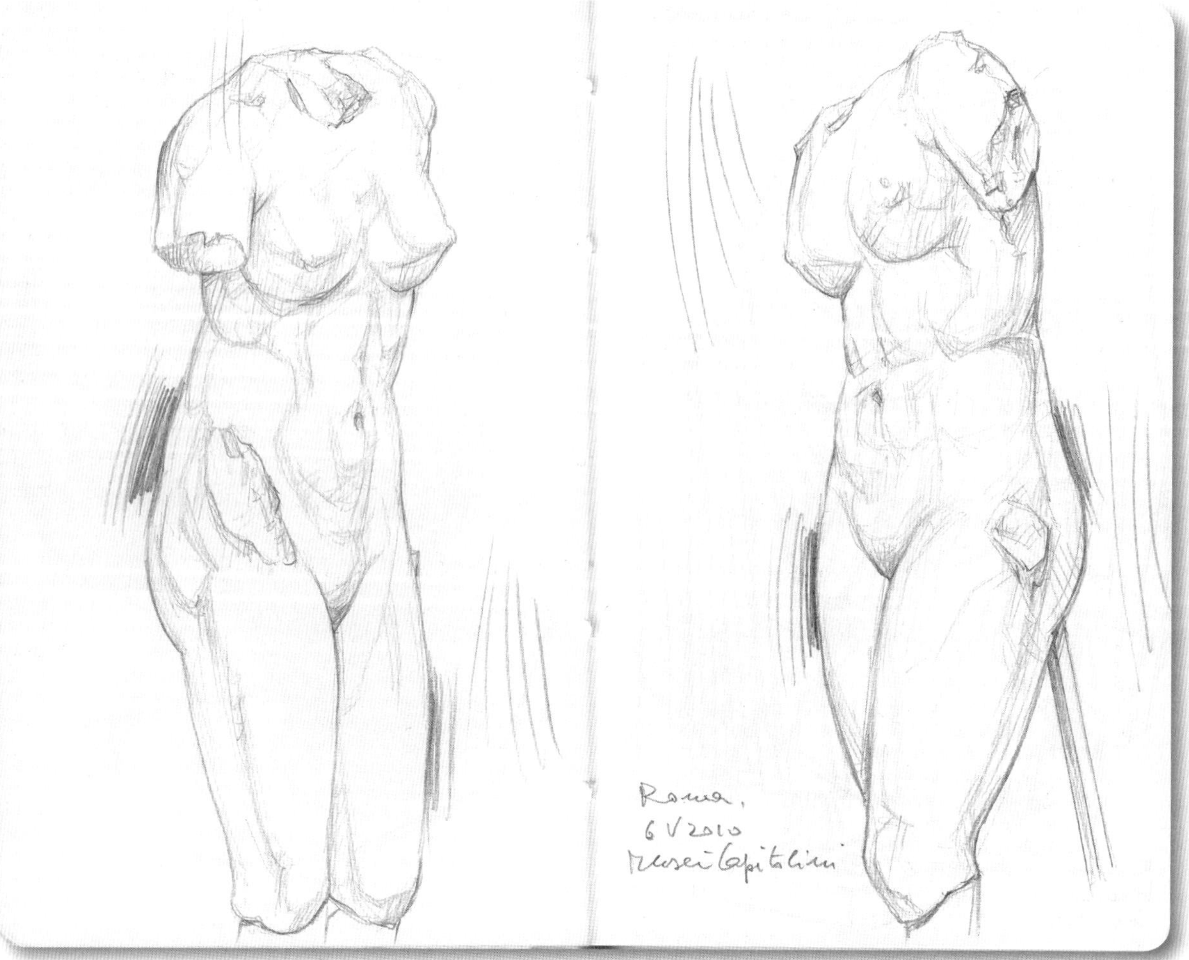
Roma,
6 V 2010
Musei Capitolini

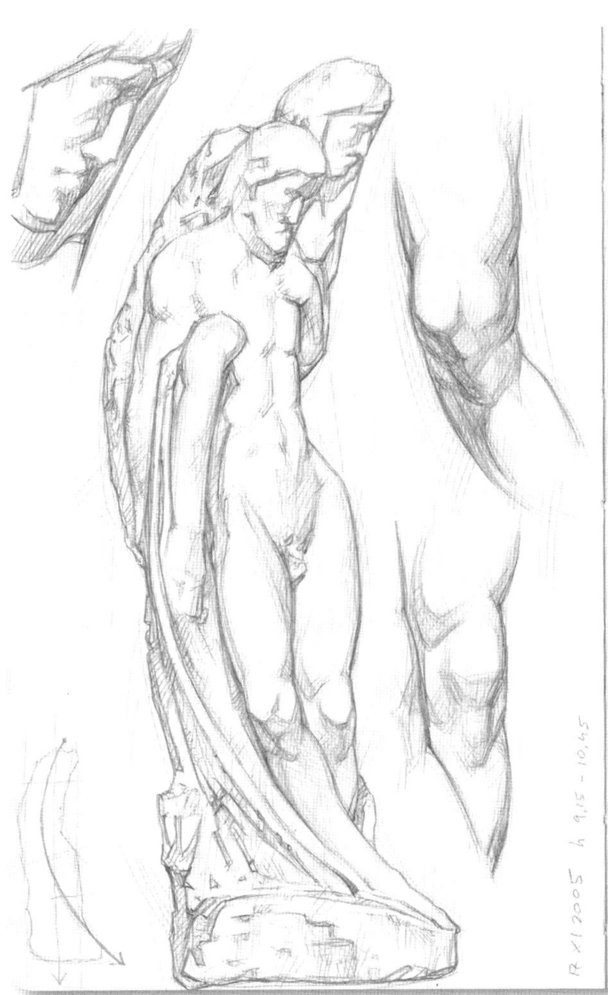

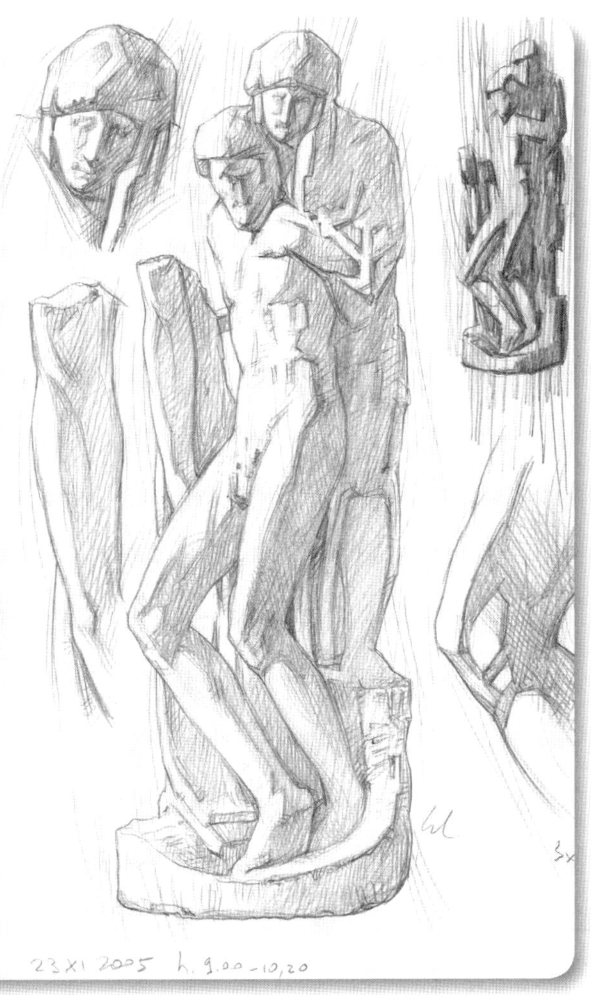

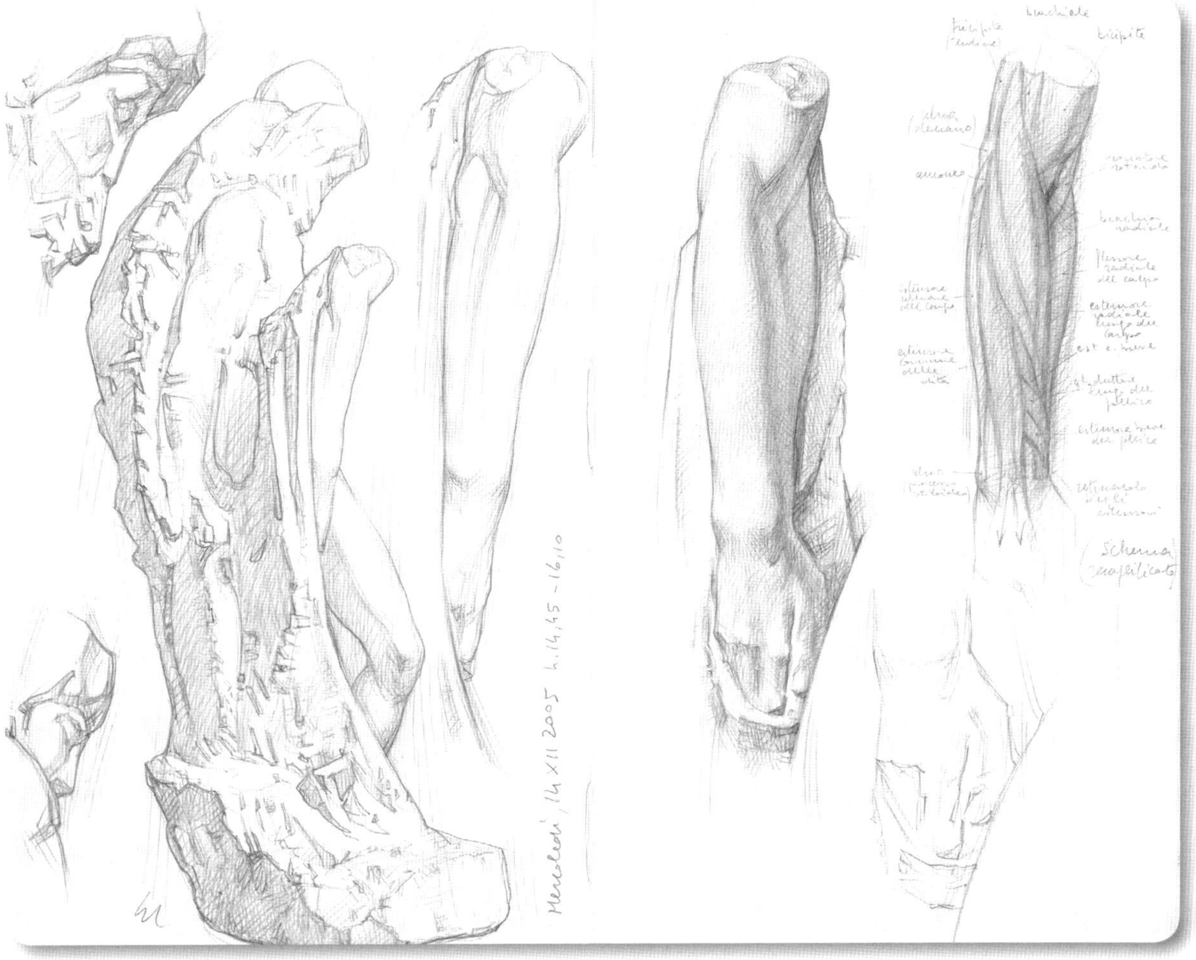

Mercoledì, 14 XII 2005 h. 14,45 – 16,10

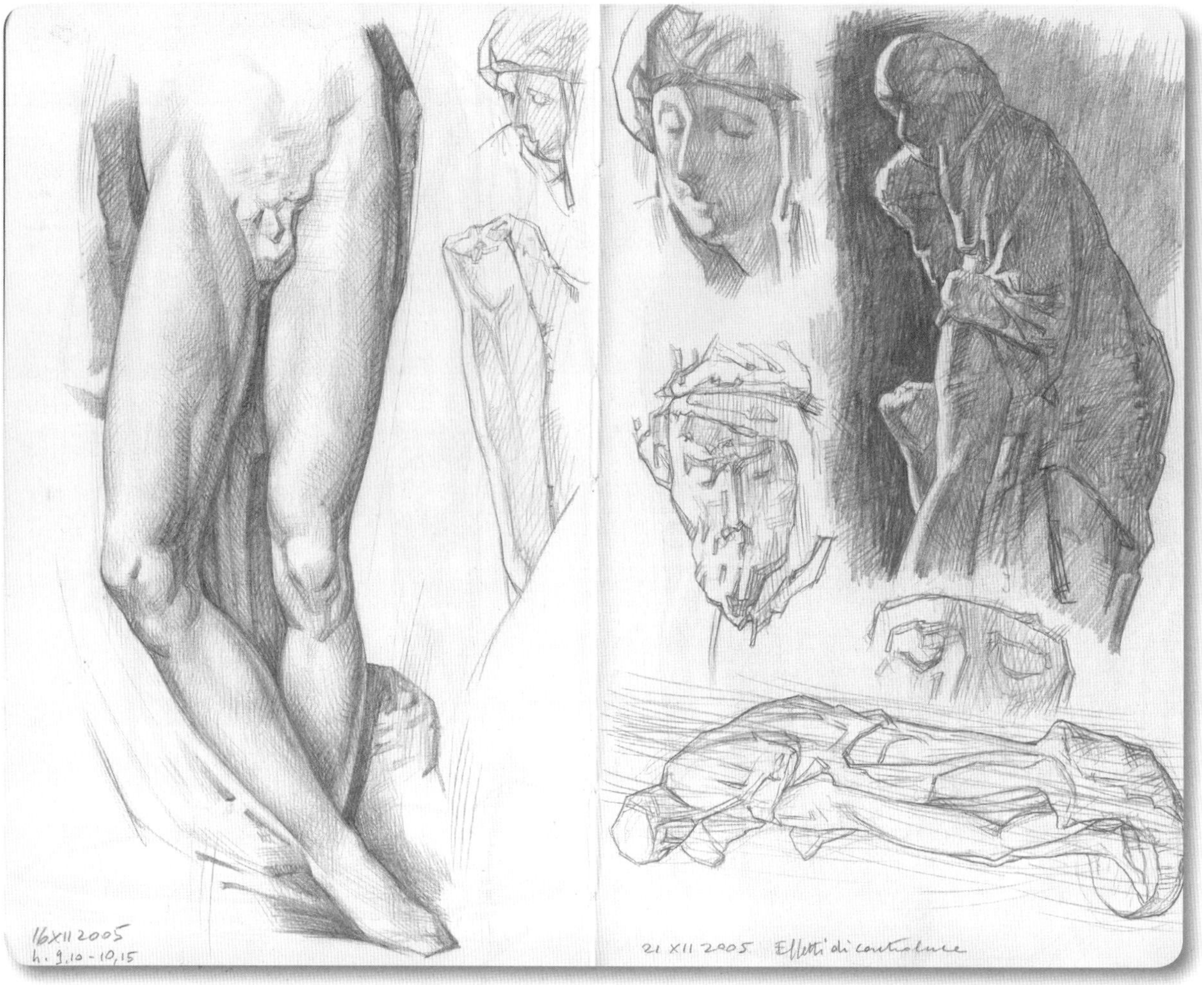

16 XII 2005
h. 9,10 – 10,15

21 XII 2005 Effetti di controluce

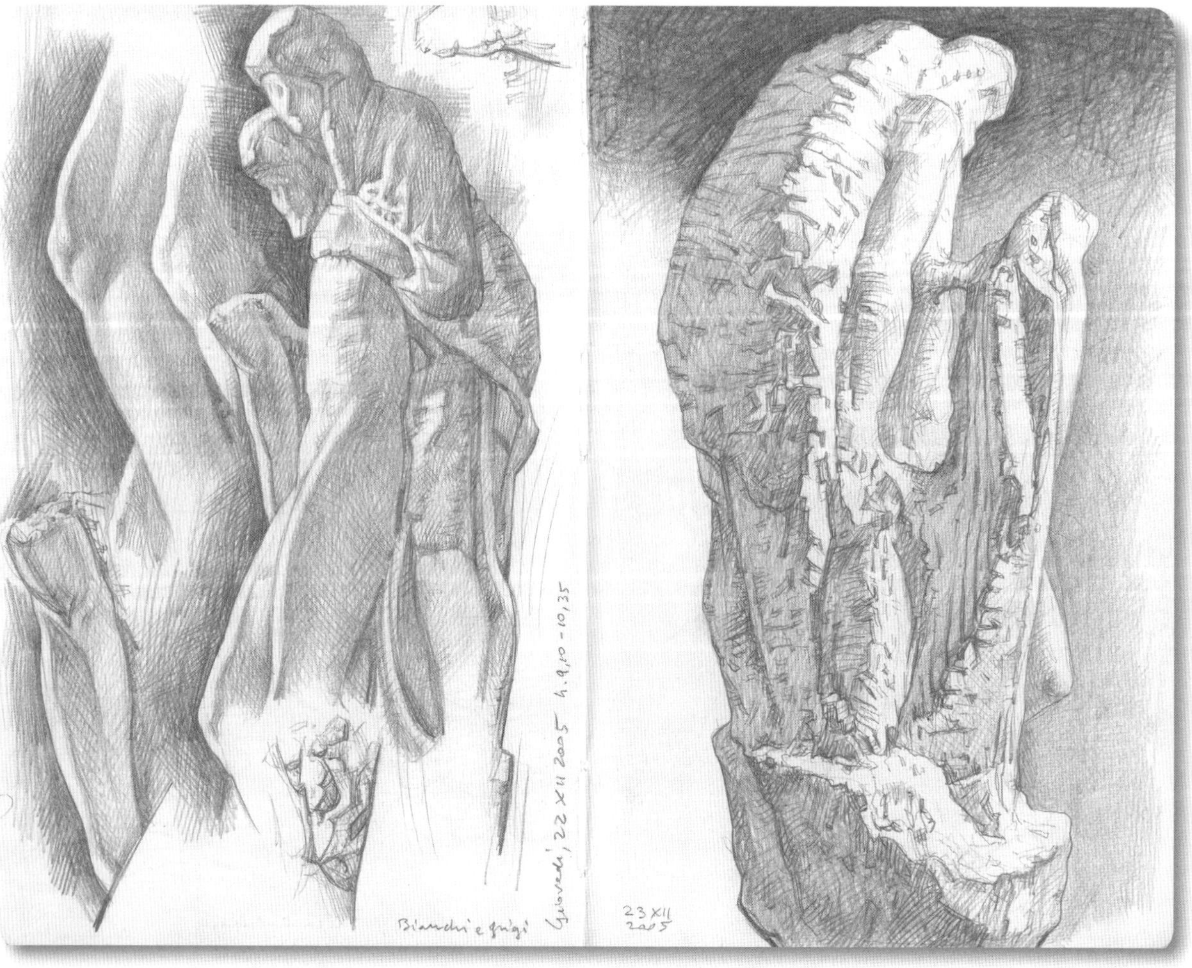

Bianchi e grigi

Giovedì, 22 XII 2005 h. 9,10 – 10,35

23 XII
2005

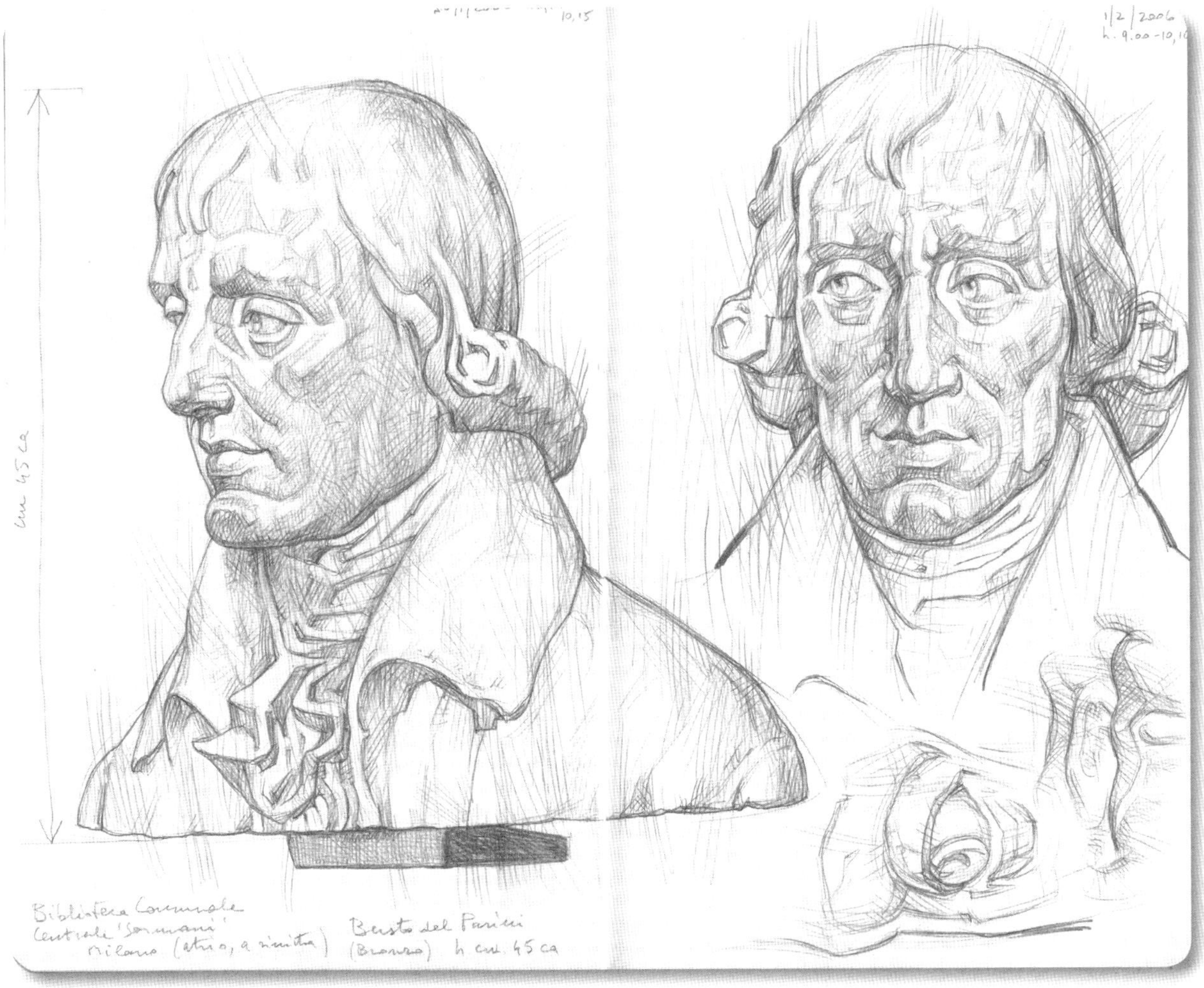

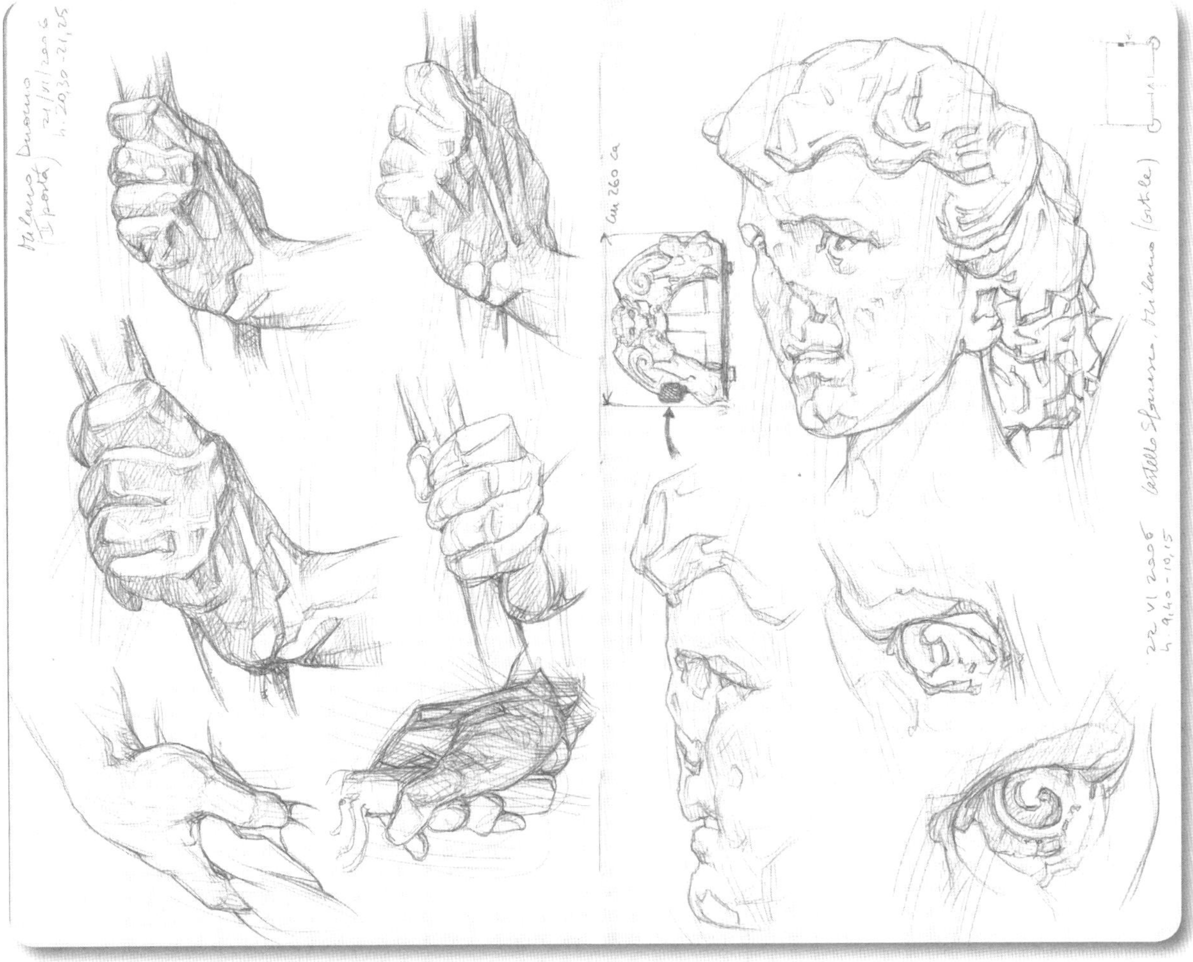

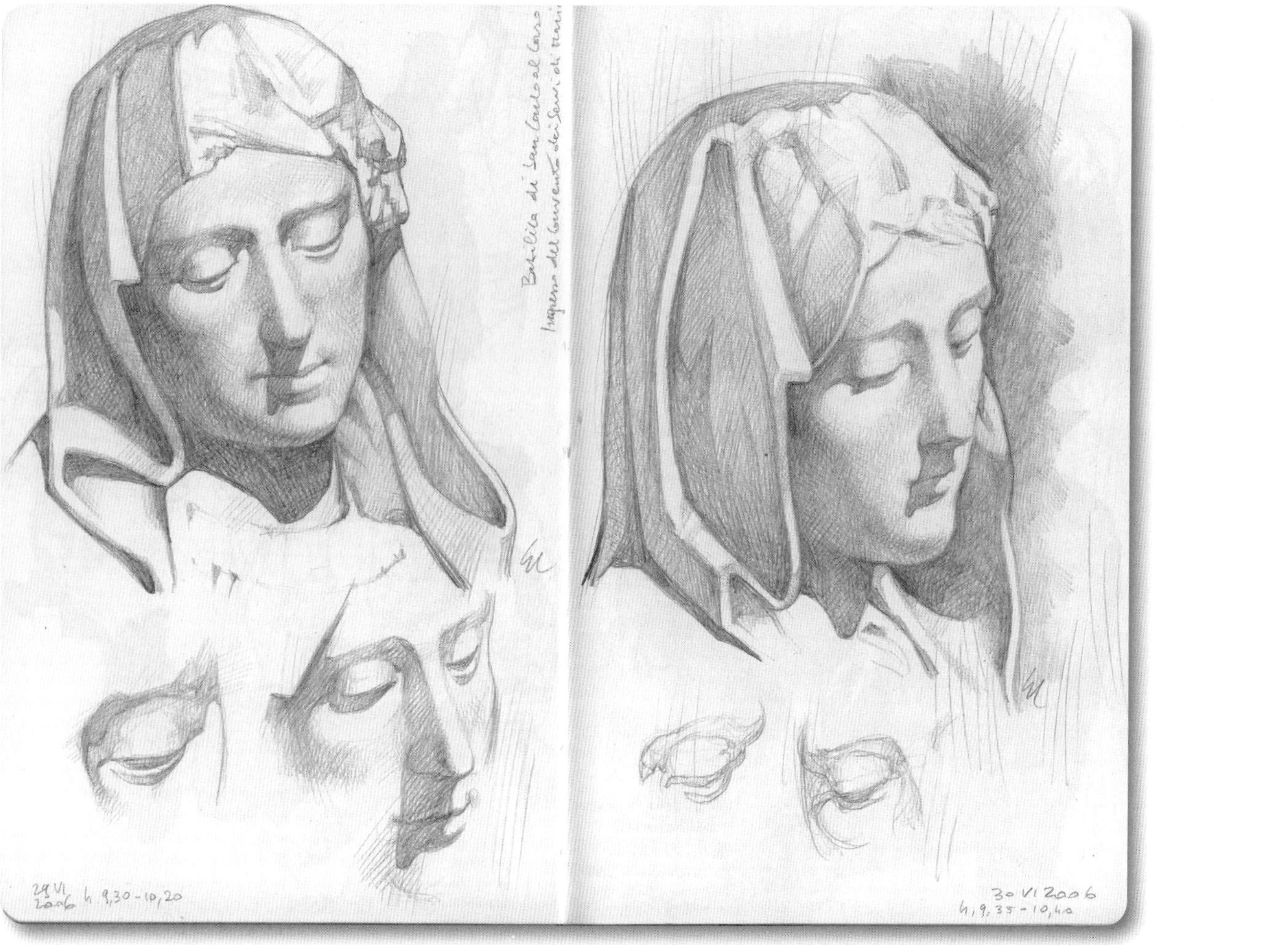

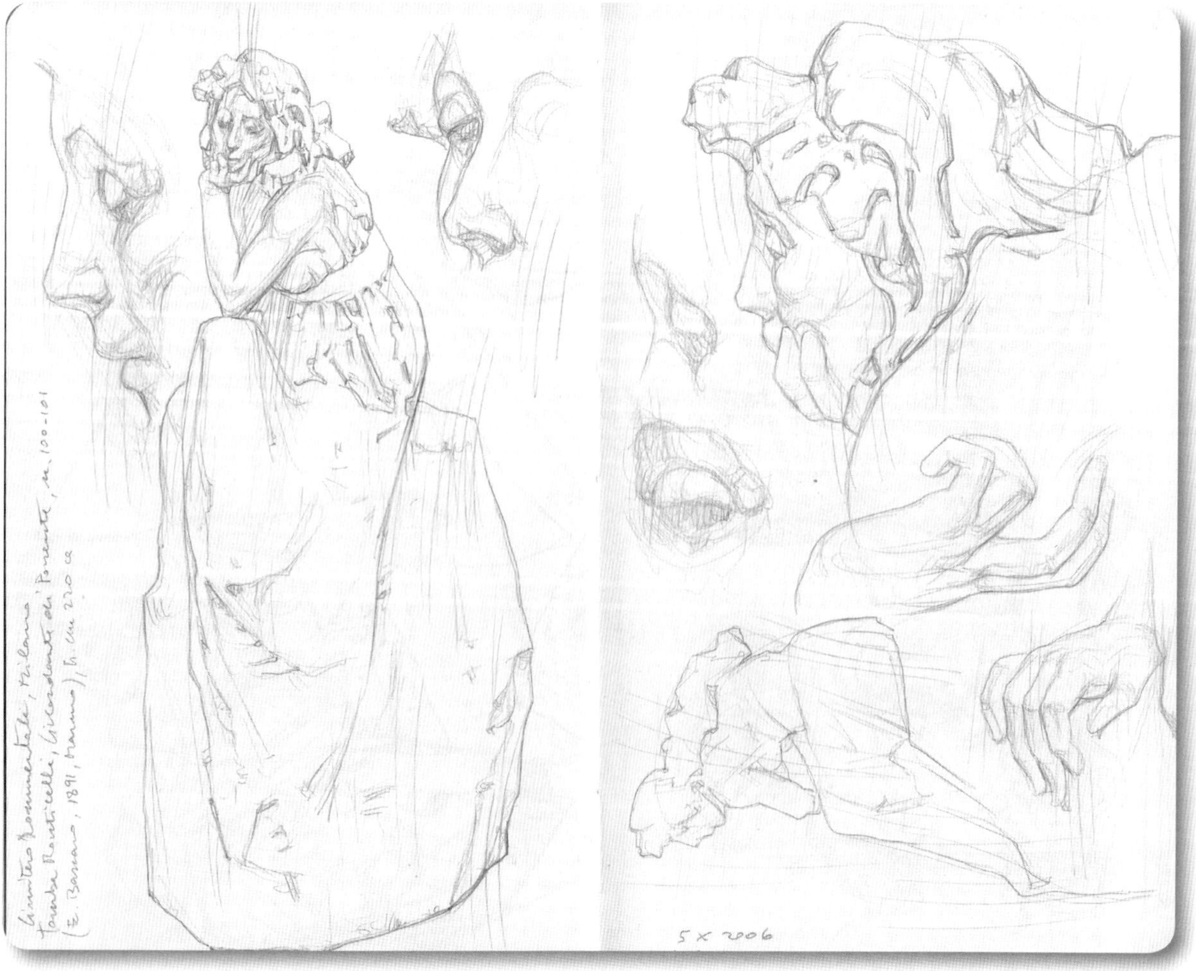

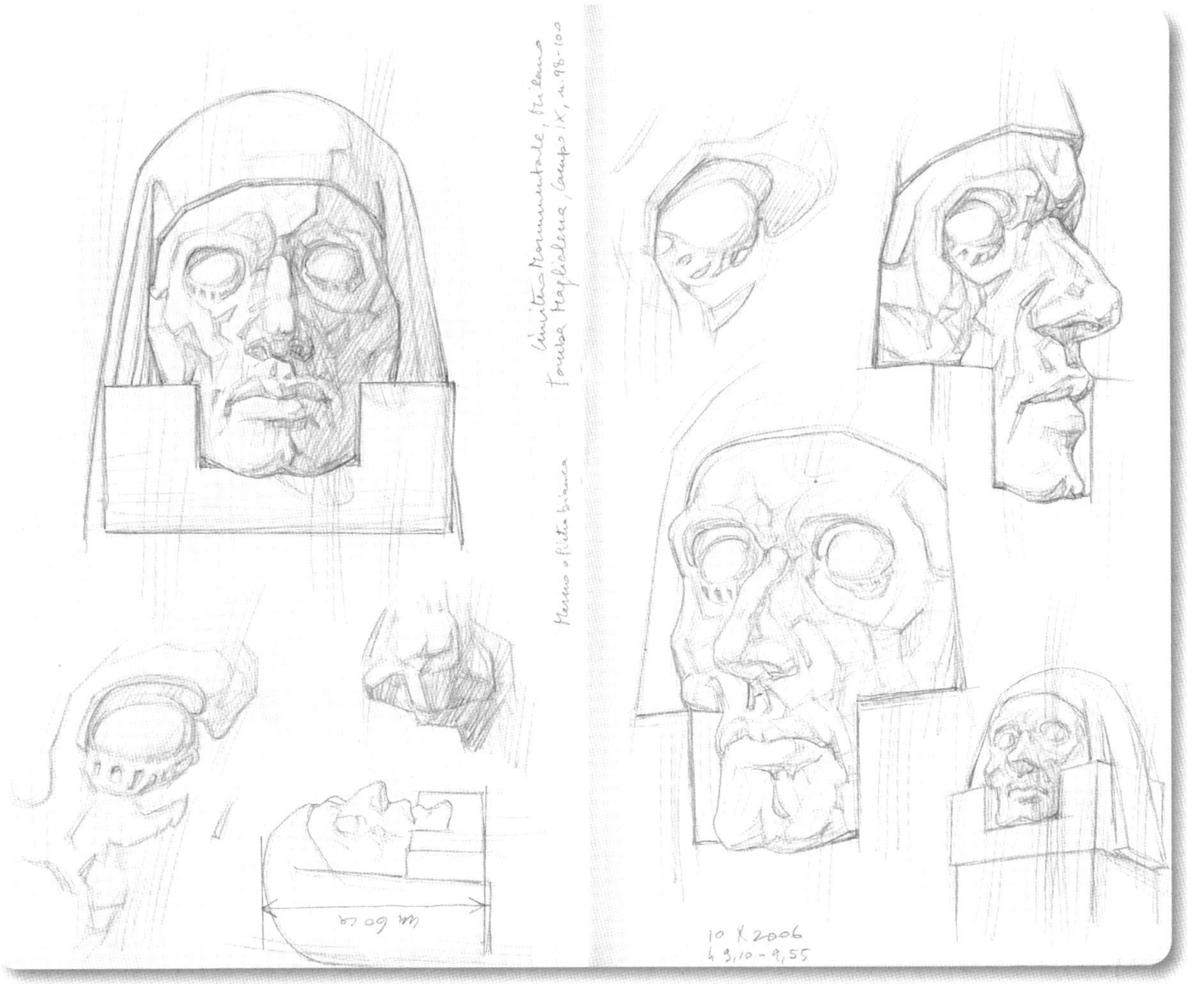

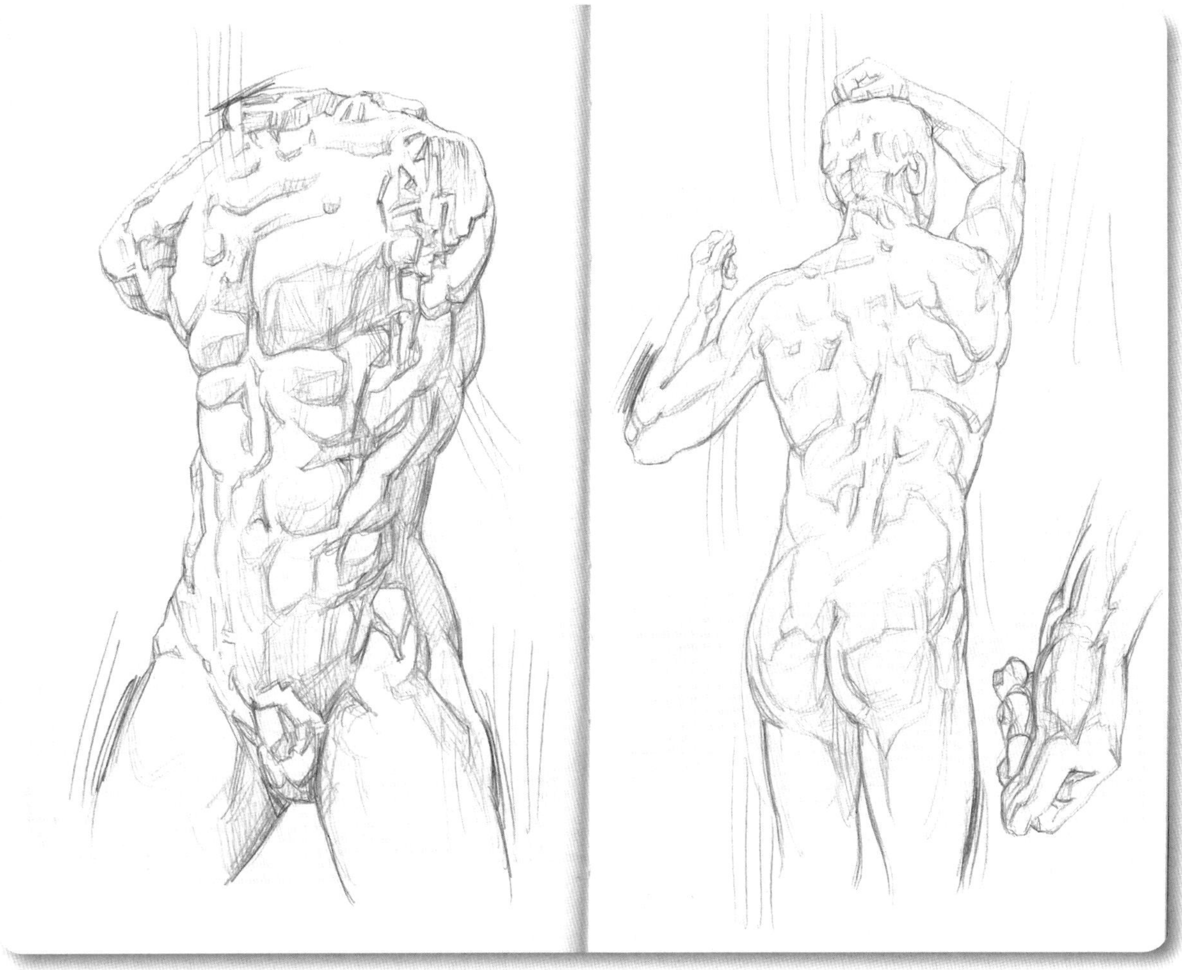

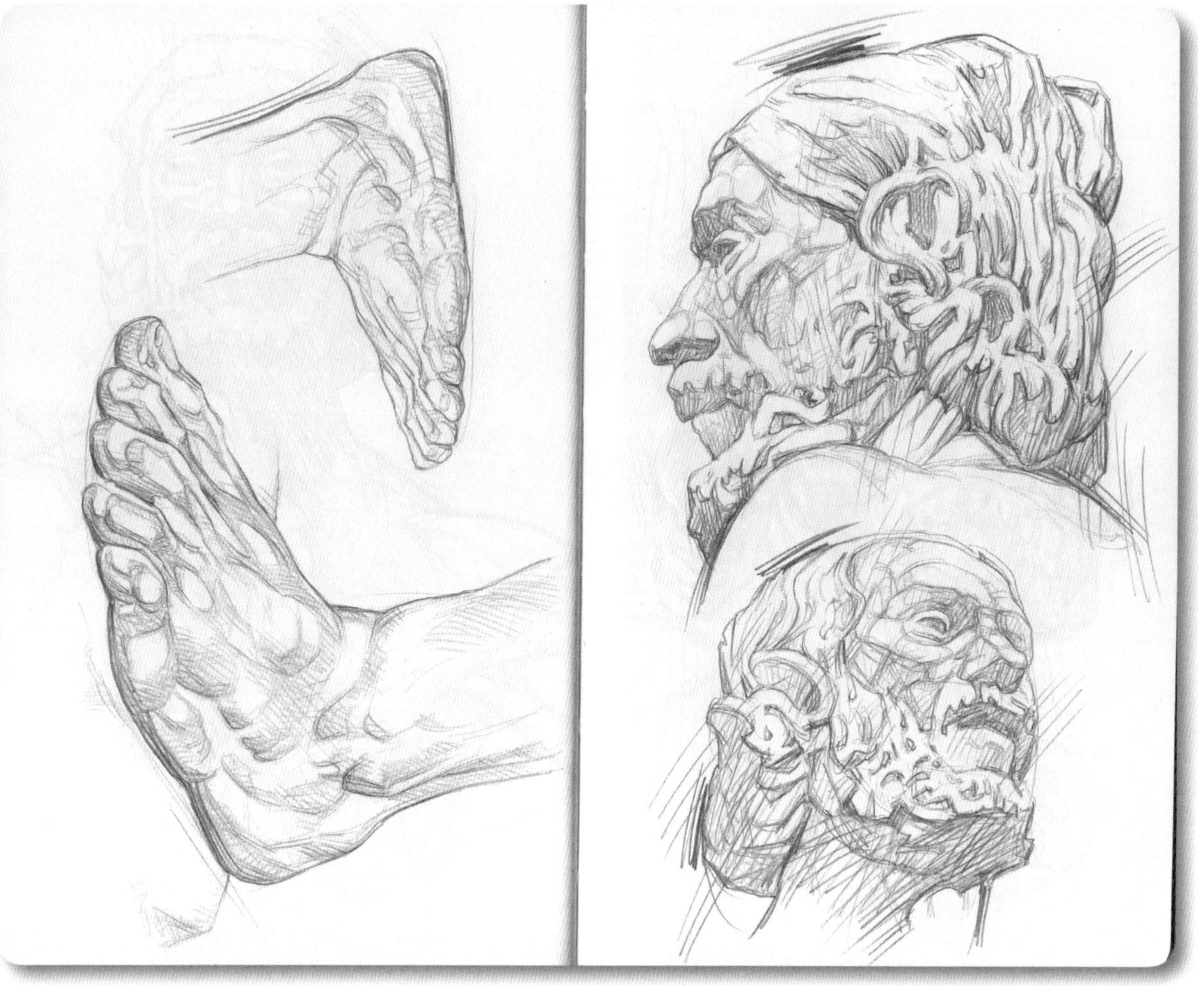

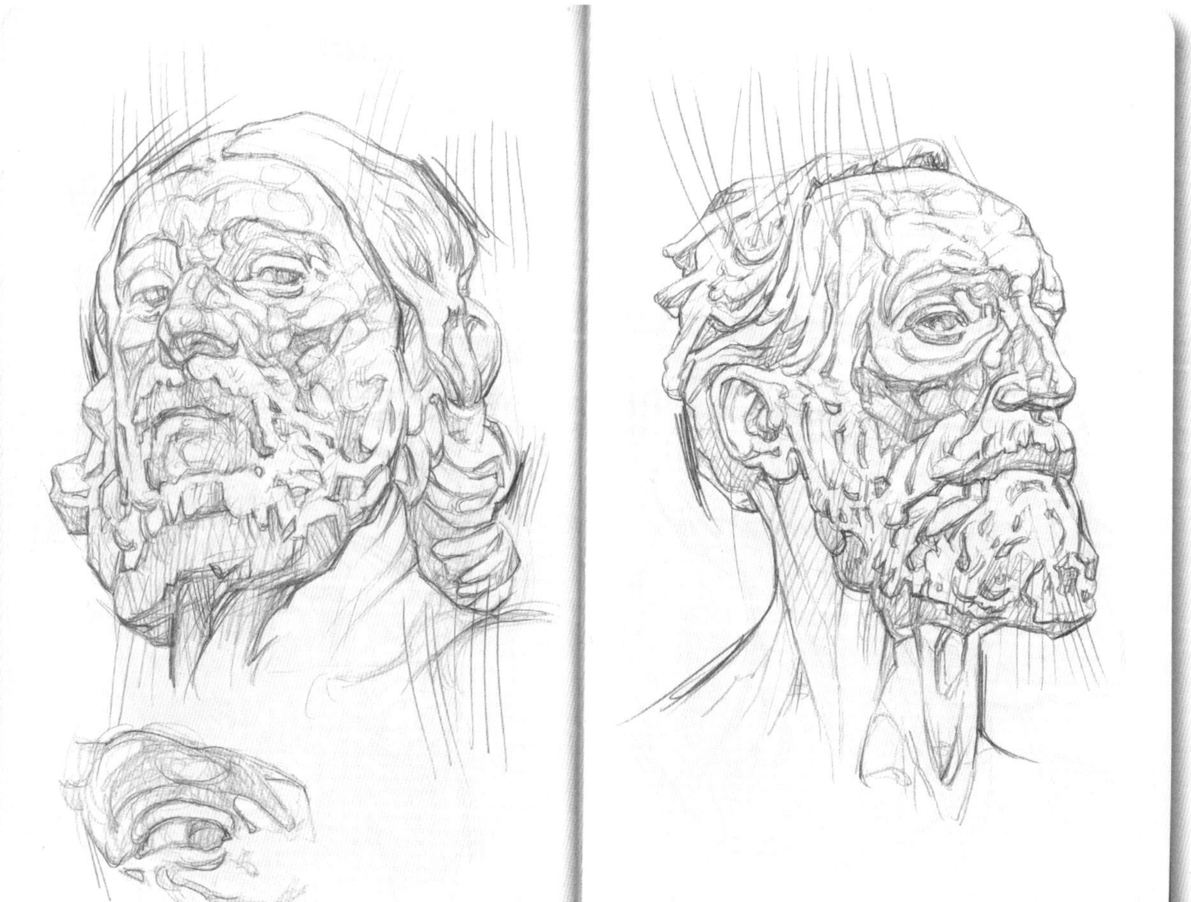

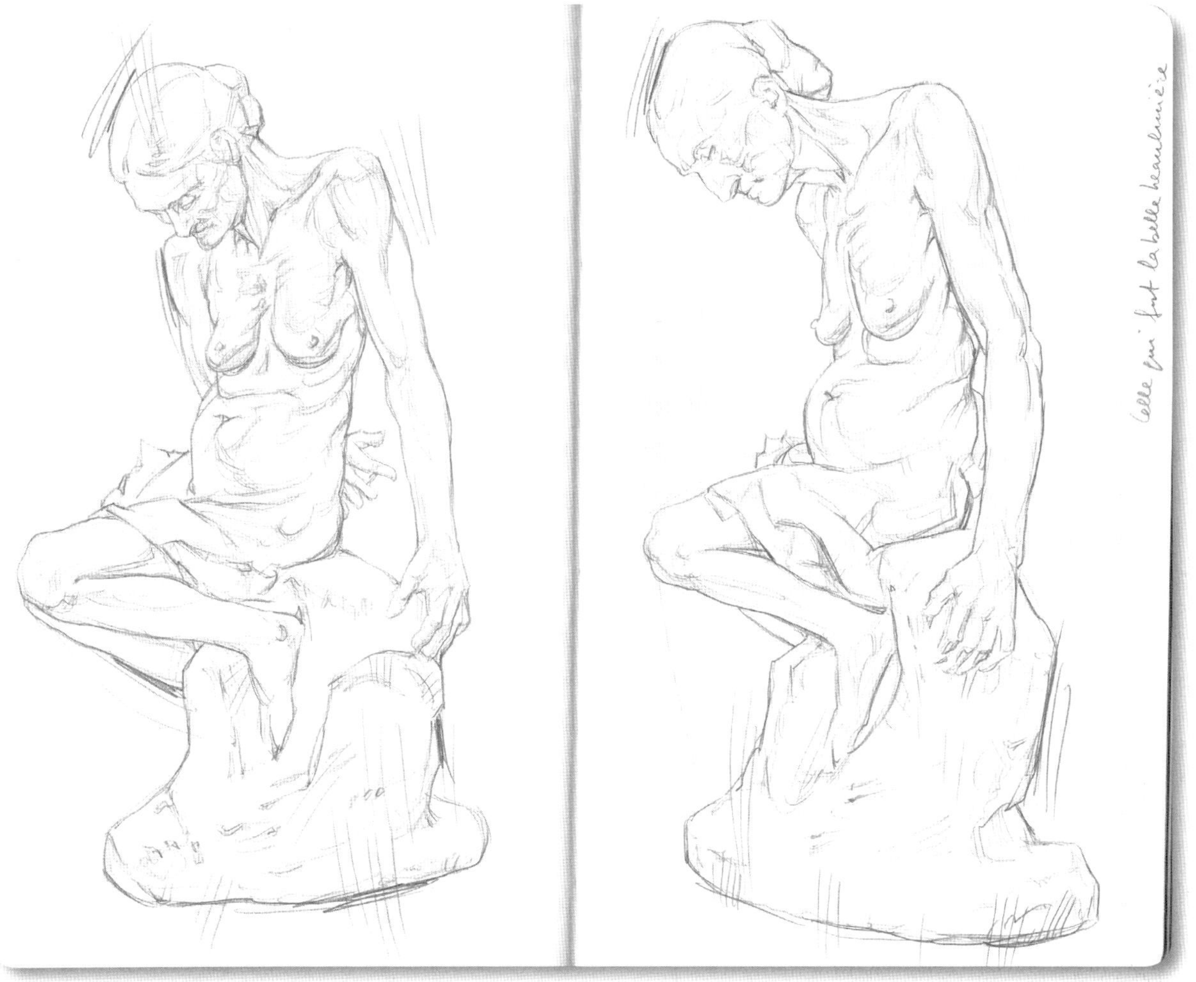

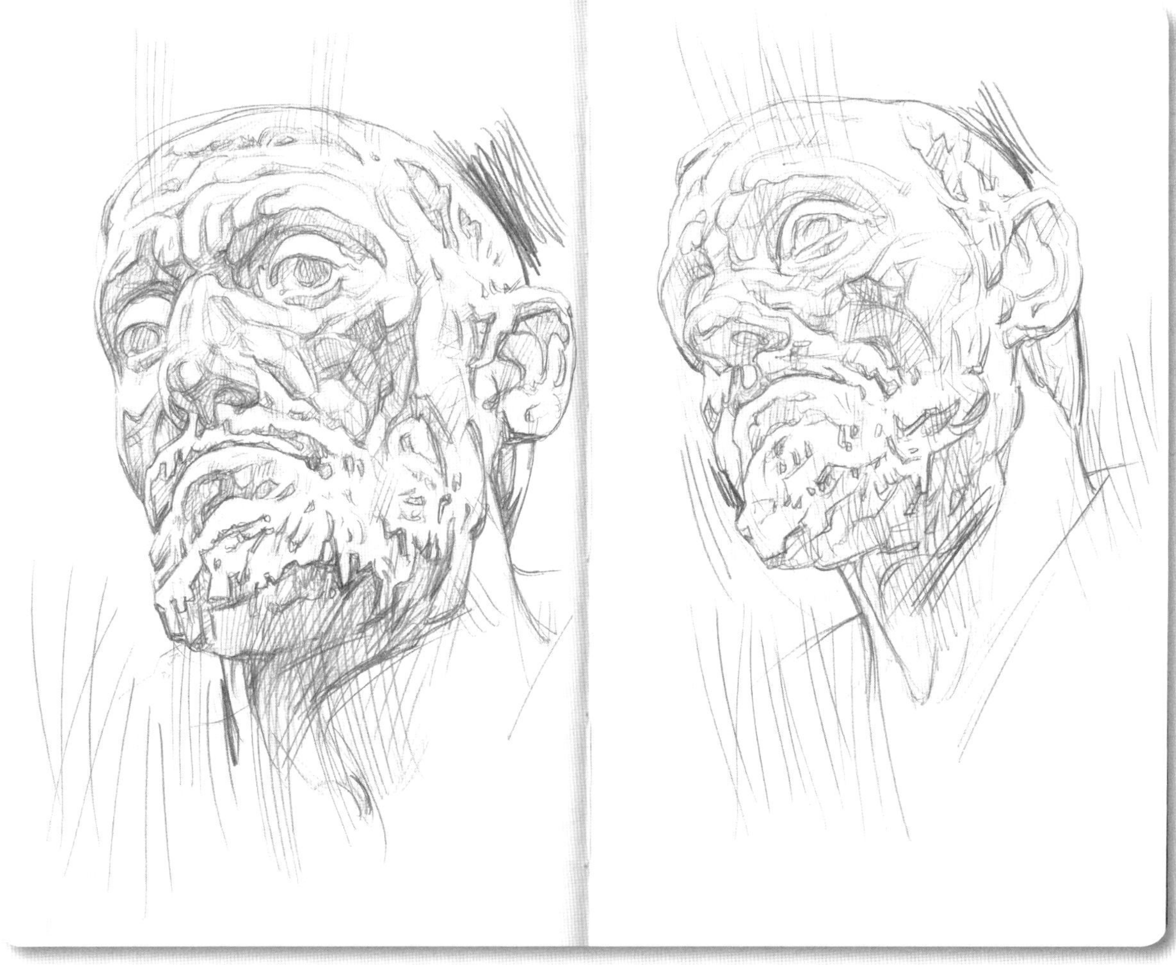

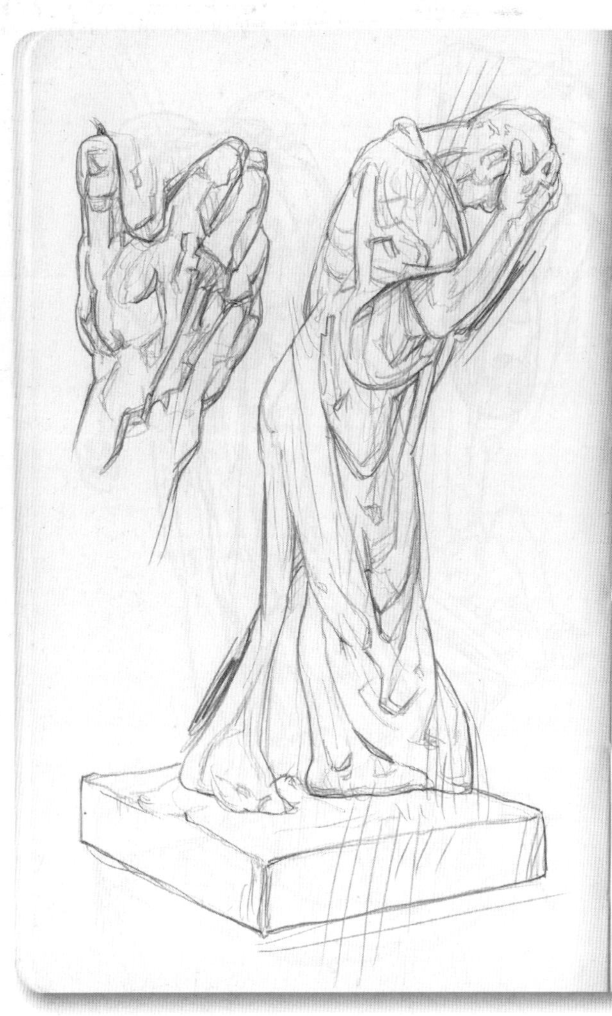

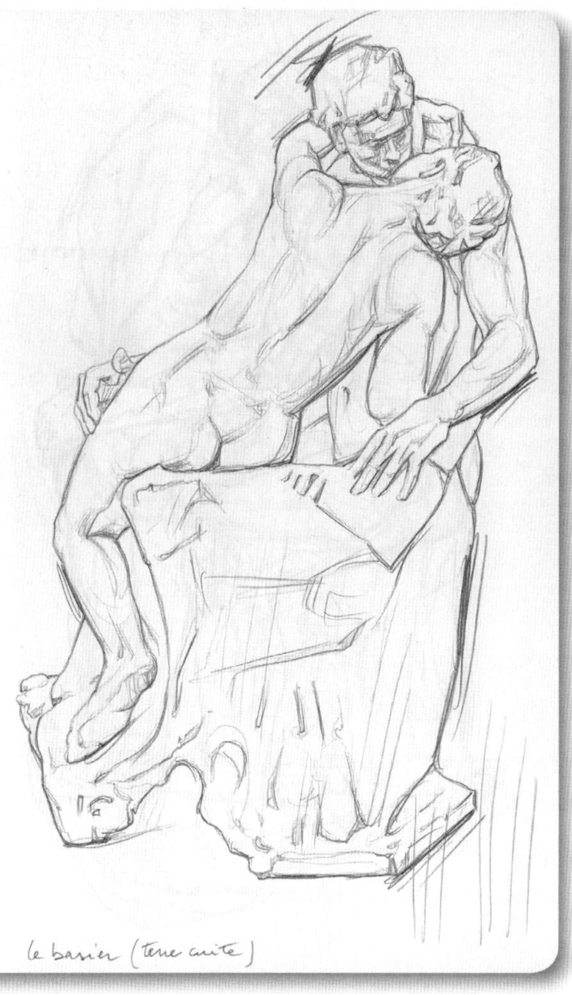
le baiser (terre cuite)

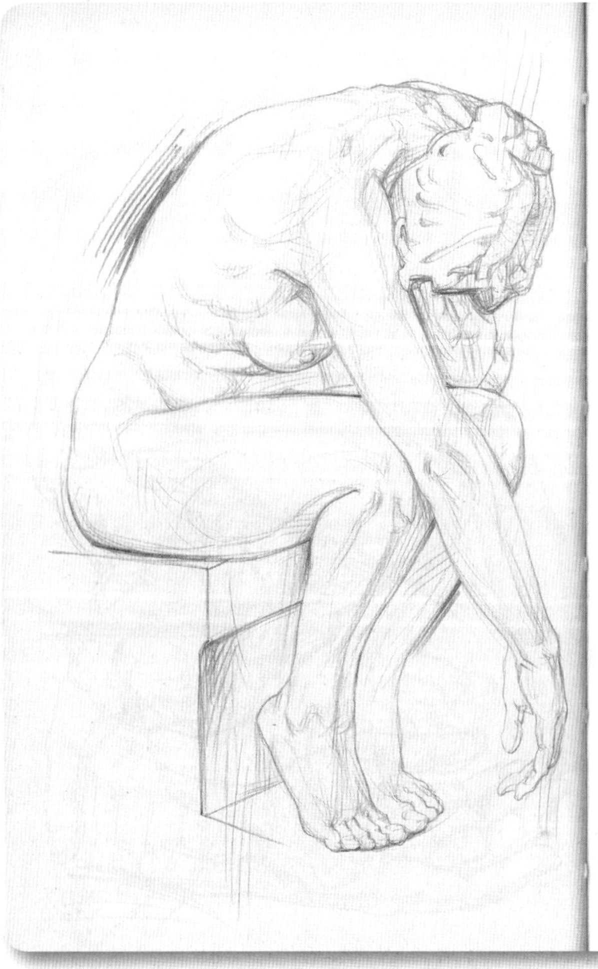

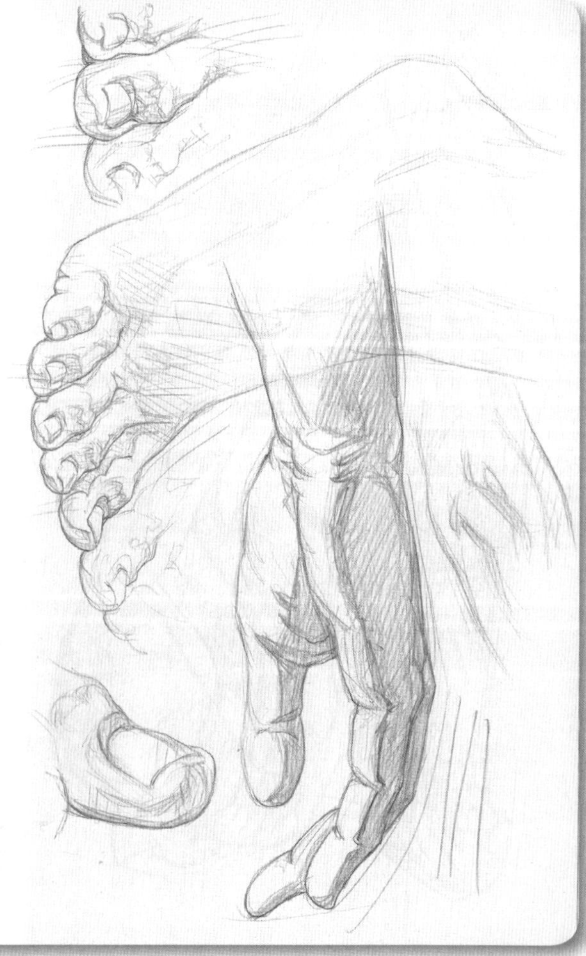